Get rea[illegible] to teach:

A guide for the newly qualified teacher

Verity Lush

Harlow, England • London • New York • Boston • San Francisco • Toro
Sydney • Tokyo • Singapore • Hong Kong • Seoul • Taipei • New De

PEARSON EDUCATIONAL LIMITED

Edinburgh Gate
Harlow CM20 2JE
United Kingdom
Tel: +44 (0)1279 623623
Fax: +44 (0)1279 431059
Website: www.pearsoned.co.uk

First edition published in Great Britain in 2009

ISBN: 978-1-4082-2039-9

British Library Cataloguing in Publication Data
A CIP catalogue record for this book can be obtained from the British Library

Library of Congress Cataloging-in-Publication Data

Lush, Verity.
Get ready to teach : a guide for the newly qualified teacher / Verity Lush.
p. cm.
ISBN 978-1-4082-2039-9 (pbk.)
1. First year teachers—Handbooks, manuals, etc. 2. Teaching—Handbooks, manuals, etc. I. Title.
LB2844.1.N4L87 2009
371.1–dc22
2009009844

10 9 8 7 6 5 4 3 2 1
13 12 11 10 09

Set by 3 in Giovanni 8.5pt
Printed in Great Britain by Henry Ling Ltd., at the Dorset Press, Dorchester, Dorset

The Publisher's policy is to use paper manufactured from sustainable forests.

For Ashley, India and Amelie

Acknowledgements

There are so many people I would like to thank! First, I would like to acknowledge the staff at Pearson, who have shown such enthusiasm and given me such encouragement – and so, to Catherine Yates and Katy Robinson, I say a huge **thank you**!

Thanks go also to the people who helped to review the book throughout the writing process: Inta Ozols and Corrinne Mackintosh.

In the years since I started teaching I have been inspired and encouraged by many people, but without Mrs Sheila Ridley, my RS teacher in secondary school, I would never have been brave enough to follow my instincts. Heartfelt thanks go to Steve Gerlach of Amery Hill School, an exceptional teacher and a dear friend – I miss working with you still! Other teachers that I would like to thank include the following: Di Horne, Lynda Kenyon, Lesley Howe, Judith Wheeden, Trudi Le Maitre, Jo Hart, Stephen Crabtree, Elaine Allen and Eleanor Abrahams. In one form or another, their advice, capacity for laughter and tales from experience, helped me through my NQT year and beyond. I would also like to thank my dear friend Loula Etherington (now Mrs Marsh!), a wonderful English teacher, who kept me laughing during our doomed Art A Level and has succeeded in doing so ever since.

This book would never have been possible without my own classroom experiences, and for some of the more memorable ones

I'd like to say a thank you to the pupils that I have taught, in particular those of Y3 (the best tutor group in the world!) and to Hannah Smith – I still treasure my leavers' book.

To my friends Al Newman and Kirsty Smith, both of whom have shown an avid interest in the writing of this book, I say thanks for the constant encouragement.

I would also like to thank my family. To my lovely mum Janet Abraham and to Grandad Lush (who has never failed to enquire as to the progress of the book!), and to my dad and grandmother, who would have loved to have seen my name in print had they been here to do so.

And of course I have saved the best until last. Thanks and love go to my dear husband Ashley, the most patient and most inspirational teacher I know. I learn something new from you every day. To our two beautiful daughters – Amelie, you kept me company throughout writing by wriggling about in my tummy, and, to India Jane, Mummy says a big 'Thank you!' You are both a splash of fun and mischief in our lives. 'All the world', poppets.

The publisher is also indebted to the following for their contributions to the book

Lisa-Jane Horrey
Mel Wilde
Lee Lewis
Roger Lowry
Helena Gracie
Rachel Ainsworth
Mike Byrne
Carolyn Myatt
Sarah Ranby
Amy Taylor
Tammy Cyngier

Contents

If the doors of perception were cleansed everything would appear to man as it is: Infinite. – William Blake, *The Marriage of Heaven and Hell*

When I was training I loved this quotation. For me, it summed up what teaching is all about. Kids' perceptive abilities are endless, and teachers are in the unique position of being the facilitators of this 'cleansing'. It's an idealistic profession – but our idealism allows us to carry on.

Or, put in less fluffy terms by someone else who was inspired by Blake's words:

There are things known and there are things unknown, and in between are the doors. – Jim Morrison[1]

We can open those doors.

Or at least hide behind one on a particularly rough day.

---

[1] Bear in mind that Morrison also said, 'I believe in a long, prolonged derangement of the senses to attain the unknown.' At times this may feel more appropriate for the kind of day you've had.

Introduction

The ten commandments of the NQT

In no particular order:

1. Thou shalt not sweat the small stuff!
2. Remember that **every** lesson is an entirely **new start** with a class – don't despair!
3. Do not reinvent the wheel: if your department has it already, use it.
4. Be consistent right from the outset – do not give an inch in your expectations.
5. Instil self-esteem in your students from the start.
6. Do not mark every piece of work in detail – save that for assessments.
7. Plan one week ahead of yourself: any more will be a waste, things change too rapidly.
8. Keep an organised diary: go through the school calendar asap and make a note of all important dates.
9. Keep yourself healthy: get rest, eat properly, you are working in a germ factory.
10. Be polite to all members of staff, including support staff: the photocopying person holds a school together!

And an extra one just for good measure: (top of page xiii)

The Timeline

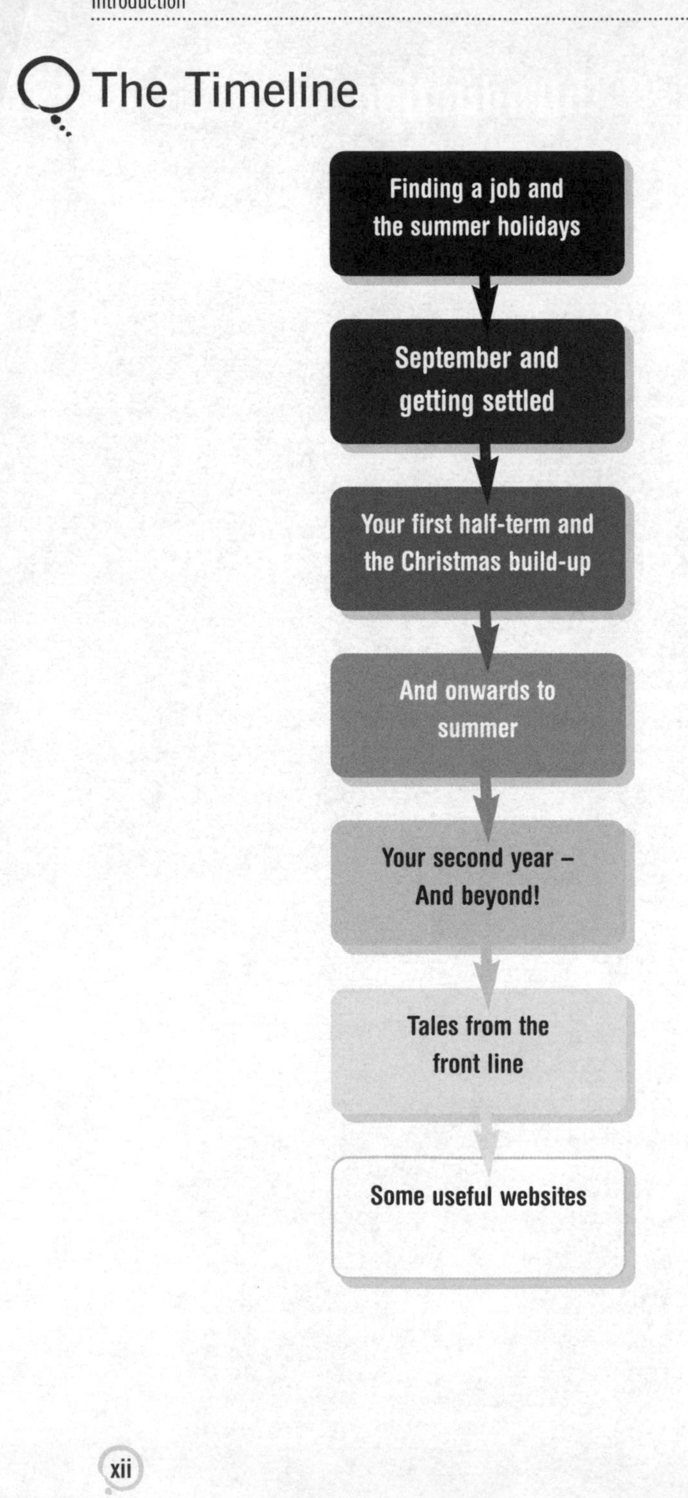

Imagine the **most embarrassing** thing that could possibly happen to you in front of a class in **excruciating detail**. Then, imagine yourself overcoming your shame and regaining control of your class and yourself.

Good. Now that you have faced the possibility you can rest assured that it is unlikely to ever happen – but that if it does, then you've already considered it and kissed your dignity goodbye. You are about to spend the next few decades standing in front of a group of mini-psychologists who will analyse your every look and murmur with an unnerving accuracy. Shame hath no place in the classroom. (Alternatively you can flick to Chapter 3 to read one mortifying example of a first full day on teaching practice. A near miss if ever there was one.)

An overview

As teachers, we seem to live our lives and plan for them by counting down between the holidays. We follow a certain timeline that other adults leave behind the moment they escape from education (or at least until they have kids), and subsequently I have planned this book around that same timeline. Each section is broken down into the timeline and contains different chapters revolving around that time of year and what you can expect – as well as what is expected of you.

Only this morning I found myself checking in my diary to see how many weeks we have until Easter: an exciting time of year, of course, because if Easter is nigh, then so is the countdown to the holy grail of teaching: the summer holidays! You will probably find yourself feeling amazed at how quickly time passes once you have entered the world of education. Terms fly by and life seems to pass before your very eyes, occasionally taking your social life with it, but always with the promise of a break soon. So, even if you have to spend that break working, at least you can do so in the comfort of your own home or garden.

Of course not every school follows the same calendar, but somewhere in this book you will find the support and advice on whichever part of the academic year you need. A brief overview of each section is as follows …

Generally you can start looking for a job as soon as Christmas is over. Aim to have one by Easter, but certainly don't worry if you do not – after May half-term qualified working teachers have missed their 3 months' notice period, so you can have the pick of any jobs that come up between now and the summer holidays.

Finding a job

The chances are that by now you will have your job – but if you do not, **read this chapter**! Even if you do already have a job, use this next time. In this chapter you will find:

- The usefulness of teacher-training placements when it comes to finding your first job
- The importance of the reputation you've built up during said placements
- *The Times Educational Supplement*
- Guidance on visits before applying for a job and finding out about the school's reputation
- The structure of an interview day
- Ideas for interview lessons
- Questions to ask at interview and things to find out – *crucial*!
- Deciding whether to take the job or not (or how to leave during an interview if necessary)

The summer holidays

Do not stress over the summer – try your hardest to relax. There are certain things that you can and should do before September, but others can wait. This chapter will give you guidance on the following:

- How to spend your time before starting and what to do over the summer (generally as little as you can, but some stuff can be sorted before you start and it is worthwhile doing so)
- Classroom set-up and personalising your space
- Sharing classrooms
- An example of the contents from a staff handbook and information that is useful for September
- Classroom organisation
- Planning

September and getting settled

Come September, you may wonder where your six weeks have gone. You may even have started your job in June and have a foot in the door already, but either way this section will act as an introduction to your first full term. You will find a wealth of information and advice in this chapter, such as:

- Information you will need (you should have been sent a staff handbook already)
- An overview of a 'typical' INSET day/s
- Things to find out before the school opens to the kids (IT systems, registers, sanctions, rewards, etc., and the people who will be crucial to your settling in)
- Performance management reviews
- Checking on NQT induction and rights and knowing who your mentor is. Join a union, if you have not done so already!
- The people you need to meet as soon as possible
- Duty teams and doing duties (break time and so on)
- Tutor groups/classes
- Your first lessons
- ICT and VLEs (Virtual Learning Environment)
- Class relationships
- How to learn names
- Ideas for rewards and sanctions

- Planning and practical lesson ideas (a great variety of really motivating lesson activities and starters/plenaries and so on)

Your first half-term and the Christmas build-up

By the time your first half-term is in sight, you may still be running on adrenalin and able to believe that this 'holiday once every six weeks' business is merely a perk of the job. By the time you get nearer to Christmas, you will have come to the realisation that it is a **necessity**! Just before or just after half-term you are likely to start experiencing more in terms of meetings, monitoring and assessment, and your first parents' evenings. This chapter is designed to help you to cope with those and also to hone your teaching skills and build relationships with the students.

- Monitoring and assessment – and how to keep on top of (not drowning underneath) your exercise books. This will include information on Assessment for Learning
- Planning and time management
- Developing relationships with students and parents (including how to deal with flirting students – a very real problem for some secondary school teachers)
- Meetings and directed time
- Parents' evenings
- Mock examinations
- Your rights as an NQT and NQT induction
- Relationships with other members of staff
- Staffroom etiquette
- Dress code
- Keeping a check on your health this term and how to set cover work

And onwards to summer

When you go back after Christmas, you will notice a huge difference in the way the kids treat you – after all, this will be your first time back after a proper holiday, when people actually know who you are – and also a huge difference in yourself. Confidence is boosted around this time, you may feel more as though you belong (and if not, then at least jobs start coming up in *The Times Educational Supplement* around February half-term). In this chapter, there will be advice on:

- Writing reports
- The options process
- Exams
- Preparing for the summer and the following September: evaluating your NQT year and moving on
- What to do if there is a problem

Your second year – and beyond!

By the time you've started your second year of teaching, you'll realise just how much you learnt in your first year. It's a vast learning curve – and, more accurately, a learning cycle that is ongoing throughout your career. In this chapter you'll find advice on how to keep evaluating your own teaching as well as learning from that of others.

- Class management in your second September
- Self-evaluation, improvement and training
- Career progression
- What to expect if Ofsted come calling
- Having a family and juggling your 'work/life balance'. (Work/life what?) This includes advice on maternity and paternity leave.

Tales from the front line

A collection of anecdotes from NQTs and other teachers. These are the kind that you tell your friends about when you actually find the time to see them.

Websites

This chapter is pretty much as it says on the tin: a collection of useful websites gleaned from a variety of teachers.

So, over to you! And, in the words of Robbie Williams and Guy Chambers:

Can I kick it?
(*Yes, you can!*)

The top five misconceptions about teachers

Advice: If you are at a party and you are new to this teaching lark, *never* mention your chosen profession in public. You have been warned.

1 You're a teacher? Cor, get all them holidays dontcha! Finish at 3pm! Call that work?
2 What do you do on INSET days? Is it like an extra holiday?
3 I always think teaching must be so rewarding – you get to make a difference!
4 So you teach primary, then? (*If you're female*)
5 So you teach secondary, then? (*You can see where I'm going here*)

The top five clichés of teaching

aka 'Phrases you will hear from the smugsters in the staffroom'

There is not a teacher on the planet who won't recognise these phrases. If, however, you are a teacher yourself and you actually *use* these phrases, put this book down immediately. It is *not* for you.

1 Oh s/he's OK – you just have to mother them a bit.
2 New teachers should know their place in school!

3 Really? (S)he works really well for me.
4 Using bad language is the sign of a poor vocabulary.

And my own personal favourite ...

5 If pupils misbehave, it's because the lesson is not stimulating enough for them.

The purpose of this book

This book is a guide for the NQT, or 'Not Quite There' as I liked to refer to myself during that period in my career (and that was on a good day – there were plenty of other times when 'Not Qualified to Teach' seemed more appropriate). Its sole aim is to provide you with advice to get you through your first year in the teaching game, to help you find your feet, and to give practical advice on how to organise yourself and become acquainted with your new school.

I first began teaching five years ago, and it was something I had felt drawn to since primary school, when I was highly envious of my Year 1 teacher's job of writing on the blackboard. First, this seemed like easy enough work to me, and second, I just loved the look of that chalk on the board. I finally began my PGCE in 2002, by which time my reasons for wishing to teach had matured somewhat – lucky really, seeing that not only are our boards now white, but we use laptops and technology to write on them. Farewell, beloved chalk.

I teach in a secondary school, and in the years since I qualified teaching has already changed a lot. You need a friend to guide you through the classroom, and, hopefully, this book will be your friend. It will tell you the truth about your first year in teaching in a way that no one else is going to until you've been in the profession long enough to see it for yourself. The book is written with a sense of humour – let's face it, if you didn't have one you'd have run for the hills the first time a student told you they could see the colour of your underwear through your trousers. It is not a profession for the faint-hearted, and one of the first things you may notice in schools is that teachers usually have a wicked sense of humour, and some of the funniest people that you will encounter will be the kids themselves.

The book will also give you real, practical tips, keeping you company as you bemoan the bureaucracy, the unsociable hours and the calendar that may sometimes see you working fifty-plus hours a week – and that's before you get home to plan and mark. If you are just starting out, then you will be entering a world where the senior managers are now referring to themselves as **leaders**. (This Senior Leadership Team is therefore going under the somewhat unfortunate acronym of SLT in many schools – meaning that some lesser mortals are referring to them affectionately as SLUTS.) There is likely to be a strong emphasis on leadership in your school now, and many NQTs themselves may be starting out their very first term with a leadership responsibility in their year group or department. This book will help you to plan your time so that you can actually stay on top of your workload. It will also give great examples of original and motivating activities and rewards systems.

In any bookshop, one can find a teachers' tome that will educate its readers about pedagogy, learning styles and methods of differentiation. These are all crucial aspects of education, but what you will rarely find is a book that will give you down-to-earth advice about the vocation, or – if you have simply stumbled into this profession because you could find nothing else to do with your degree – the job. It will tell you how to build relationships with other members of staff as well as the kids, how to set up your classroom and make a real impact, how to deal with flirting teenagers, when to sort out your class lists and how to muster the energy to make your way through to your first half-term – all illustrated with real anecdotes from real teachers. What you won't find is acres of script about the philosophy behind education. You've done enough of that at uni, and although your mentor or professional tutor will have told you that your training year was the hardest – they lied. As all Not Quite Theres soon learn, the hardest year is the first. The one where there is no one to whom you can pass the buck, where you are stuck with the classes you encounter in your first week for the **Whole.Entire.Academic.Year**! Argh! Yep, that's right. They're all yours. Including their GCSE/SATs results at the end of it. It's enough to make anyone scared, especially if you remember some of your own behaviour from your schooldays and the nicknames you had for your teachers. Well, those nicknames are yours now – and so is the responsibility!

Too many teachers feel alone when they experience that pervading sense of doom just before 9Z4 bounce down the corridor towards them, e-numbers buzzing round their hyperactive grey matter and an air of lunacy in their eyes. Well, rest assured: **You Are Not Alone**! Read on, take comfort, and, in times of total classroom turmoil, remember that number four in the top cliché list is just a pile of b******s, really.

Just on the off-chance that you're reading this and don't yet have one...

Chapter 1
How to find a job

This chapter will offer advice on the various issues associated with finding a job. You can go about this process almost from the September before you qualify, or you can even leave it up until after the May half-term. Generally, people will start searching some time after Christmas.

- Teacher-training placements
- Your reputation
- *The Times Educational Supplement*
- Guidance on visits before applying for a job
- Finding out about the school before you apply
- The structure of an interview day
- Ideas for interview lessons
- Questions to ask at interview and things to find out
- Deciding whether to take the job or not
- How to leave during an interview if necessary

If you are reading this book, the chances are that you are either qualified or approaching that crucial time, and within a hair's breadth of grasping your QTS certificate in one hand and a copy of *The Times Educational Supplement* in the other. Unless you are one of the hundreds of would-be teachers who drop out of their PGCE/GTP/QTS course during the first few months of training, you are presumably planning on finding a job at the end of these gruelling months. You may have had the kind of day in the classroom that leaves you wondering why on earth you would want to, but the monumental debt left by your student loan is probably enough to have most of us clamouring for our copy of the *TES* on a Friday morning.

I was so desperate after some days during my PGCE that I actually started buying lottery tickets. It wasn't until I bumped into an old friend from uni – who had already qualified – that I realised I wasn't alone in feeling so stressed at the end of a bad day. She said that she had wanted to quit numerous times during her PGCE but stuck with it. She became a Head of Department in her NQT year and says that teaching was the best decision she had ever made. I kept this in mind every time I felt low and am so relieved that I did – qualifying and finding your own job is fantastic!

There are several ways in which to go about finding your dream job in teaching – and I would suggest that you combine all of them and, most importantly, think **very** carefully. However (in the words of a story that is now the subject of many a news article on whether or not Nativity plays should still be allowed in our schools), **be not afraid**! There are so many things to bear in mind and so many schools to choose from, but the chances are that you will find the one for you – and if you don't, it's never the end of the world. (Coincidentally, I can think of at least thirty teachers from my university who found their first jobs at the school/s where they had their placements – which speaks volumes about the importance of where you are placed and your reputation whilst you are there.)

Teacher-training placements

Your absolute key and therefore door opener to finding out where you want to teach (and actually landing your first job) begins with your training placements. You will – or at least should – be told by your university mentors to 'submit and comply' whilst on practice. Keep your lips firmly sealed about your opinions unless or until you know for certain that you are well out of earshot/wide-angle camera lens of **anyone** who may bear even a passing resemblance to a person who works at the school in question, or even attended it as a whippersnapper. The following cautionary tale should make it crystal clear why this is so:

I knew of a boy who had been training at a school and was on his second placement. At the pub in town he sat in a booth chatting with his mates and merrily launched into a full-on tirade about the school in which he was now training in comparison to the one he'd just finished at. He went on to explain in minute detail exactly where the Head was failing and even went so far as to graciously point out the many physical failings of said Head. Alas, the person sat in the booth behind was the brother of said Head – and the boy didn't even manage to land a job in the same county after that, let alone either of the places he'd trained at. – A professional tutor in West Sussex

---

Your reputation

You can never be too careful about who you are speaking to and who they know – or, indeed, who is eavesdropping. You will be amazed by staffroom politics when you first join a school and it doesn't end there. It may not seem like it, but you'll have been building a reputation from the very second you walked through the door – and that reputation is going to precede you wherever you go. A substantial number of teachers really do find their first jobs at one of the places in which they have at some point trained. By keeping your head down, working hard and fitting in, you not only impress people but you get to see how that school works. You suss out the ethos of the place and you can begin to feel at home.

This is not to say that I don't remember sitting in the staffroom of the place where I taught my first ever lesson and simply thinking 'Oh God, no!' on the morning of my first full day there. I was terrified at innumerable stages during my placements and often thought very seriously that I wished to run back to the checkout at Waitrose and hum 'Nine to Five' until I could bugger off home. At times I just didn't want the responsibility and I didn't want to spend hours planning plenaries at home; I wanted to leave it all behind at the classroom door. Every so often I felt as if I would never cope, drowning instead beneath a sea of paperwork and planning. Luckily I found out that most of my contemporaries from university felt pretty much the same way at first. I kept plodding onwards and soon enough fell into the rhythm of organisation that I still stick to now:

1 **Plan one week ahead.**
2 **Keep an organised diary.**
3 **Take it day by day.**

At the end of my PGCE year, my first placement mentor retired and another vibrant and dedicated teacher took over her Head of Department post. He interviewed me for his previous position and

I landed the job, so beginning my teaching career as a Newly Qualified Target. I went on to spend a blissfully happy four years at that school, it was a great time, and I can honestly say that I do not have one unhappy memory of working there. The staff and the kids were fantastic. An amazing start to a career – and I wish you the same. It just goes to show what can come of your training posts.

The Times Educational Supplement

websites

www.tes.co.uk

A doddle to use: just type in your area and the position you're after, and whether you're primary or secondary.

www.eteach.com

Another useful website to browse during your search for jobs.

The *TES* is a marvellous thing and is indispensable to all who are job-hunting in the teaching profession – as is the *TES* website – because here, from the safety of home (or the staffroom/classroom if you're being sneaky), one can read with excitement about the possible jobs that are out there. I say 'safety' because of course when you are merely reading the *TES*, you are not actually **out there**. You can look past the euphemistically phrased 'challenging environment' and see it for what it really is: a zoo that hands out armour plating to all staff at the front gate and has a staff turnover of sixty-plus a year. You can then snigger merrily to yourself and skim read on to the much nicer-sounding 'well-disciplined', 'high-achieving', 'centre of learning' and so on – but you will never really know what you are reading about unless you have first- or second-hand trustworthy experience of the school in question. In fact, you may want to work in a place that is 'challenging' at best and zoo-like at worst. You may be up for the challenge, buzz and extreme motivation that can come from teaching a group of disaffected teenagers to actually sit in chairs for longer than ten minutes at a time, or helping a dyslexic five-year-old to try and write their own name for the very first time. Either way, you need first to find a job advertisement – and then you need to **visit**! I repeat, **visit**.

Before you apply for a job

Do not go for your interview at a school you have not yet stepped inside or do not have insider info on. Of course, this may be impossible if the school is miles away, in which case there are other options that we will come to later, but unlike almost any other job on the face of the earth, teaching is one where you are offered the job **at interview** and you will be expected to give your answer **at the same interview**! Therefore, **take your time, be fussy, do your groundwork, ask questions**.

Interviews

The *TES* comes out on Fridays – but the website is updated all week long.

Assuming that you have sent off your application form and been asked for interview (and never underestimate the advantage of having a teaching practice mentor to pester for help in this area if you need it), then the average interview day at a school runs pretty much the same no matter what establishment you are attending. This is a point that you can clarify with your current mentor. They will be able to tell you how an interview would be run at their school and can give you excellent ideas for the lesson you need to teach. The title or subject that you need to base your lesson around will be provided by the school itself – which leads us to what is possibly the most daunting part of the day . . .

Ideas for interview lessons

Sometimes you will not be expected to teach an entire lesson; it may be only twenty minutes, which can prove harder rather than easier. Ask your mentor if possible for advice and take it on board, then make sure that you prepare well in advance: resources can take time to create. Find out if the classroom you'll be in has a projector/laptop available and so on – what is at your disposal? However, do not fall into the trap of preparing and expecting to do too much. You don't want to try out your newest most experimental approach and fall flat on your posterior during this period – save that for when you're back at your placement. Some ideas for top-notch interview lessons are as follows:

- Keep it **simple** but effective.
- Ask the school for **information about the class**, including age, ability and even male/female ratios.
- If you are teaching an entire lesson, ensure that you have a **captivating starter, contemporary resources for main activities, and an impressive plenary** – in other words, a plenary that works. Ideas for all of these may include Image Enquiries, Sorting Cards, Community of Enquiry, music clips, video clips – but nothing too complex that may go wrong on the day. If you don't know a class or the room you're in, then a Vote with your Feet may go horribly wrong, and things like cutting and sticking have little place in the interview classroom (see Chapter 4 for some excellent activity ideas).
- Use **ICT** where possible. Never make the fatal mistake of reading out your PowerPoint slides. Instead, use them to **facilitate** teaching and learning. Check whether you need to take your own laptop or just a memory stick. Ask if there's an interactive whiteboard or if the kids have their own laptops. Make the most of what you know how to use, and forget anything you are not competent with.
- You can write the kids' names on **stickers** and hand them out (or you can give them blank stickers, like yours truly did, and

they can write 'Jennifer Lopez' and 'Minnie Mouse' on them), but do bear in mind that they can muck about with them. It is amazing how many kids give into the temptation to attach them to their heads and backs – and the last thing you need is to emerge from the trauma of teaching an interview lesson only to enter the Head's office with a sign saying 'Kick me' stuck between your shoulder blades.

- When asking questions, **ask them their names** and try to remember some. Make a connection.
- Use your **sense of humour** as you would in your usual lessons – though bear in mind that you don't know these students the way you do your own.
- Stick to your usual style of **class management**: things like making sure the kids look smart at the end of the lesson and that they are silent before they leave can help to show off your management skills when you only have a short amount of time in which to impress.
- Try your hardest to **relax** – you've been teaching for a while now, and after all, this is just another lesson. You'll be so accustomed to being observed by this stage that the interviewer sitting at the back of the room should make no difference to you. Hold your head high and teach your socks off!

tip Do a practice drive or journey to the school and plan your route and timings carefully, judging such factors as traffic and road works. Check on parking and so on.

The structure of the interview

You'll be given a schedule of the day, usually in the post at the same time as the interview offer, and the average day runs like this:

- Arrive, meet the Head
- Teach a lesson

- Have a tour
- Possibly get quizzed by some kids: student voice is, quite rightly, taken very seriously in some schools. (In fact I had to teach a lesson to a class just to get on to my PGCE course and they were all asked afterwards what their opinions of me were. Yikes!)
- Have lunch and meet members of the team
- Face the panel (the order in which interviewees are grilled depends on the number of you there and the school in question. Occasionally a school may actually leave the person they are most impressed with until last and tell the other poor souls along the way that they are unlucky this time. Others have no order at all – so just relax at this point and prepare to ask your own questions, which leads me to my next point . . .)

tip **Have an interview lesson back-up plan. If the lesson relies on ICT and the technology doesn't work on the day, you need to know you can still teach the lesson.**

There are many things you do not need to be told about interview days: you know by now how to dress for your interview and you realise that you're going to have to teach on your interview (if not, be suspicious about what kind of educational establishment you are landing yourself in here). However, do bear in mind the importance of asking your **own questions** during the interview. In a sense, you are going to have to interview these people to find out not whether you are the right person for them, but whether **they** are the right people for **you**. Remember, once you've accepted and signed that contract (which some schools have been known to actually pull out from a clipboard/desk at the precise moment a potential employee says 'Yes please' to a job offer), you are stuck. As I've already mentioned, you'll get offered the job on the day – and you'll be expected to reply immediately.

The following little tale is a cautionary one. The general advice here is that you need to know something about where you are going on interview before you get there. I shall reiterate the point made earlier: **do your homework**!

At the interview we had lunch in the sixth form centre and I taught a delightful group of top set Year 8s. Things couldn't be better! This week, my fags, phone, lunch and purse were nicked from my room. When the charmer in question was caught trying to flog them at break in the playground, I was told that he couldn't really be punished as we had no proof he actually took them. The sixth form centre lunch and Year 8s flashed through my mind again that afternoon during one of my lessons where another boy told a girl (delightedly) that he could 'smell her a mile away'. She (quite rightly) went mad, and I (quite avidly) read the *TES* on my way home – English teacher (third year of teaching).

Now, if you do accept such a job, it is not of course the end of the world. However, it is seen as particularly bad practise in teaching to move around too much. In first jobs for example, the expectation is that you stay put for at least four or five years. Again, this all comes down to building your reputation. As an example, an English teacher I knew of had worked in her first job for *less than three months* before finding another, such were the people skills, staff retention and leadership qualities of her first head of department. (In fact, according to rumour, the teachers at the head of department's previous school held a huge leaving party for him once he got his new post, they just neglected to invite him.) Subsequently she left her first school in a hurry – however, the problem truly arose when a promotion (in the shape of a head of department position) was then advertised almost immediately at a fantastic school where her best friend worked. This was a bigger department and nearer to home and she couldn't resist going for it. Clearly this was a little bonkers – she had barely stepped foot in the door of her new staffroom. Instead of thinking of what a foolish career move this might be due to the effect it could have on her reputation (due to lack of staying power in a job), she wrote out yet another application form and was called to interview. In her excitement and haste she told her new Head of her plans. Alas, New Head was not Happy Head – and in the cold light of day she realised quite what a daft career move this would be. Three jobs in your NQT year alone is extreme and not a very good idea at all. She immediately cancelled the interview, annoying both schools in the process and some members of staff there. To be fair, she has since managed to re-build her reputation, but she could just as easily have blown it: teaching is like a *vacuum*, everyone knows everyone.

tip It may be an idea to take a copy of your CRB check (Criminal Records Bureau) with you, and even your QTS certificate if you have it. Exam certificates are also useful if you're offered the job.

Questions to ask and things to find out

Hopefully it's obvious that these are **suggested** questions. Some may not apply to you, and some may not bother you – but all of these are crucial information that you will need to find out at some point. Whether or not they will make or break your decision is down to you. Some of these apply just to secondary/primary, some are relevant to both.

1 Whereabouts on the **pay scale** will you be starting?
2 Is it a **foundation school**, or will you be employed by the **LEA**? (Usually the latter, but you can come unstuck in terms of childcare vouchers and so on if it's the former.)

3 How is INSET dealt with? (Some schools run **twilight INSETs** so you stay late at night but break up a bit earlier. You may prefer it this way or you may need to juggle family evening commitments.)
4 What about **PSHE**? Does the school run focus days or similar, or will you be expected to teach PSHE? If so, when and how often and who plans it?
5 Will you have your **own classroom**?
6 If you have a **tutor group**, what year group will they be and will their tutor base be in your room or are you expected to relocate for registration?
7 How often are students **assessed** and is this is a whole-school policy or is it departmental?
8 Are **registers** paper registers or computerised?
9 Will you get a **laptop**?
10 Who will be your **mentor**?
11 What kind of **induction programme** is there?
12 What is the **homework policy** and how often are you expected to set it? (In one school where I taught, we were expected to set this online and were actually checked up on weekly. A list was then sent out saying who had/had not complied.)
13 What are the policies regarding **sanctions, rewards,** etc.? How will you be backed up in class by your Head of Department etc.? (Think back to the tale of the fags and phone being nicked – there is a school where staff are not supported!)
14 How many **meetings** are you expected to attend and for how long?
15 What **extra-curricular** activities will you be expected to take part in or run, and how much scope is there for you if you wish to start a new club and so on?
16 If you are in a secondary school, how are **options** dealt with? (In some schools these are now known as 'Pathways' and students receive a coloured sheet depending on what their Year 7 CAT results were. Each sheet has different options, ranging from one that allows you to take any subject to one that only

offers construction or something similar. According to your principles as a teacher, you may agree or disagree with this. There will be more on this in Chapter 7.)

Of course, this list could go on and on, and hopefully you'll have thought of a few questions of your own to add – but, in general, these are some important ones to include in your interrogation! And, importantly, they have been gleaned from experience.

How to leave during an interview if necesssary

Last, but certainly not least: it is important to bear in mind that you **can leave the interview** before you even get to the stage of being interviewed. This is particularly useful if you have no knowledge of the school or have had to travel miles to get there and have not visited before. It takes a serious amount of courage to explain to a school politely that you have no desire to work there, but then it takes a serious amount of courage to stand up in front of unpredictable kids day in day out and try to teach them (when both they – and you – would sometimes rather be elsewhere). Obviously you need to turn down a job as courteously as possible and use all the diplomatic skills at your disposal. It may seem as though it would be easier to feed a cookie to Posh Spice than to teach your interview lesson and then explain that you are buggering off, but it would be even easier to teach political correctness to Jim Davidson than to schlep into a school you loathe each day for the foreseeable future. If in doubt, leave. Do so politely (reputation, reputation, reputation), but leave. The great thing about teaching is that when you find the right job, you will want to get up in the morning, you will love the place where you work, and you are going to do the best job you can possibly do because you'll **want to**. Happiness is key: yours and the kids'.

If you are successful – celebrate! It's pretty much a given that you need little advice on this front. Although, as the majority of interviews for NQT posts do not take place on a Friday, do bear in mind that teaching with a hangover is **vile**!

Remember – all schools open over the summer. Just give yours a ring beforehand or look on the school's website to check times.

Chapter 2
The summer holidays

It can be difficult to know what you should prepare before you start at your new school, particularly when you don't know what to expect. This chapter gives advice about the summer holidays and whether or not you really need to do anything before you start back in September:

- How to spend the summer holiday before you begin
- What to do in advance and what not to do
- Classroom set-up and personalising your space: primary and secondary
- Advice on sharing classrooms
- Classroom organisation
- To plan or not to plan

The summer holidays may seem as if they will stretch on for ever – or they may seem as though they are going to fly by in the blink of an eye and that all too soon you will find yourself walking through those school gates. A certain amount of nerves can be a great thing, it can be really motivational, and hopefully you'll be feeling a great deal of excitement too. If however you are feeling terrified, remember that you are not alone! It can be incredibly daunting starting a new job – **any** new job – let alone one that requires you to deal not only with adults (who may or may not be on your wavelength whatever line of work you are in) but with such unpredictable creatures as children and young people. In fact, as this example goes to show, whatever your position is in a school and however long you've been teaching, the thought of a new term is enough to make even the most experienced among us have a quiver or two:

Every September I go through the same thoughts – can I really do this? Then, a couple of days later, I find I've just slipped back into it again without even really noticing. – A Deputy Head who has been in the profession for thirty years

---

No wonder, then, that those lesser mortals among us who have not yet reached the heady heights of SLT find our stomachs churning over our cornflakes on 1 September. However, at least those nerves show that you **care**: at least for your own sanity if not for the students that you've yet to meet. There is nothing worse than a smug and arrogant teacher, be they SLT or NQT. We all have something to learn in the classroom. At the end of the day if thirty students wanted to stand up and tell you to get lost, then they could. I once observed a PGCE student teach her first ever lesson by introducing herself as having studied at Oxford University. Had the very young and very low-ability kids in front of her had a clue what this meant, then I am pretty sure that they would still not have been impressed – as it was, they immediately picked up on the fact that she appeared to be telling them that she was better than them, and promptly began giving her a hard time. However the trainee had meant to come across, it was not a successful move.

tip Relax and get away from it all – September will come round really quickly! Make the most of a holiday that's free of marking whilst you can.

How to spend the summer holidays before you begin

Presumably you have just spent the toughest year(s) of your life slogging away at this teaching business and trying to familiarise yourself with a profession that surely has more acronyms than any other on the planet (QCA, Ofsted, HIAS, SACRE, anyone?). Having finally reached the finishing line then of this monumental learning curve, you deserve some rest. Try to get away for a while and take time out completely from teaching. As all your friends will probably have told you by now anyway, we teachers are horrendous bores. God forbid you live with another teacher – you'll talk about nothing else. Thankfully my husband is a primary teacher, so we at least have different tales to tell in the evening. By the very nature of our students and their ages, my tales usually revolve around fights or teen pregnancy scandals; his usually revolve around incontinence incidents or boys trying to show girls their willies in the toilets. Clearly there is a toilet theme going on here! (And also a willy one, bearing in mind the latter secondary school example.)

So, if you can manage it, slink off somewhere for a bit, switch your teaching head off, and enjoy the break. The key to the summer is, that if you can relax, then do. The benefit of doing so is that your mind separates itself from teaching for a bit. By doing this, the same kind of thing that happens when you learn to drive occurs without you even realising it: one day you need to think about **everything** you are doing and **why** that is, and it's all a blur, and the next day, it has suddenly clicked without your even noticing. It's an almost imperceptible shift from brain-overloaded novice to competent teacher, who automatically uses a plenary and differentiates with VAK whilst understanding why they are doing so, and without even realising that this momentous shift has occurred.

What to do in advance and what not to do

> **tip** There's no need to get carried away with planning until you know the kids: too much will change and you'll have wasted time.

It can be very tempting to get a bit carried away over the summer. Occasionally a rogue thought may enter your head that attempts to convince you that you could plan your entire academic year over the summer holidays, fully resourced and good to go, thereby saving yourself hours of pressure and an insane work schedule in September. Or, on the other hand, you may be reading this from the opposite end of the spectrum as you laze on the beach for the fifth week running, having forgotten what your name is, let alone what 'QTS' stands for. Either way, the answer as with most things in life, is 'moderation'. And the general advice for the summer holidays is, as Frankie says, RELAX. You'd be wise to do some preparation but, for several reasons, there is no point whatsoever in going overboard – it will be a waste of time.

The following offers some sound advice on **things to sort before September** if you feel that you must.

You should by now have a **staff handbook**. This is usually posted in advance to NQTs and new members of staff as is it published in school by the late summer term. This will often include the school calendar (which you can write into a diary now or wait until September when you should be given your teacher's planner), and lots of policies and waffle. These will generally revolve around things such as what the school's sanctions and rewards system is. What can be interesting is to see where your name pops up. For example, you may find assembly lists and who is taking them, the names of classes/tutor/form groups and who they belong to, the SLT structure and so on. This does not make for a riveting read, but my current staff handbook includes the following:

tip **Whatever age your kids are, get a vast supply of STICKERS ready for September. Eventually your department should give you some, but it's best to be prepared for your very first lessons.**

- School improvement plan
- Self-evaluation
- Policy statements
- Rewards and sanctions
- School rules
- Full staff list
- Full list of governors
- Expectations for staff
- School organisation
- Leadership team responsibilities
- Year Heads, tutors, codes and names
- Duties
- Wet weather arrangements
- Break and lunchtime arrangements
- Support staff line management
- Performance management structures

- Fire points
- Services to the school
- Emergency procedures
- The calendar
- Dates for the school year
- Assemblies
- Detention rota
- Records of achievement (aka reports)
- Teaching and learning policy
- Home school agreement
- PARS registration system
- Minor repairs and maintenance
- Cycling regulations (Yes, really)
- Accidents
- First aid provision
- Minibus
- School visits and out-of-school activities
- Accounting procedures under Foundation status
- School plan

So, a pretty extensive list there. Also a list that you can ignore in general until you get started, but for those control freaks among us, you may wish to have a snoop and see what's what.

Classroom set-up and personalising your space

This is crucial for secondary and primary teachers alike, although if you are primary then it will take you more time, and not just now but throughout the year. My husband spends umpteen hours on his class displays, and I'm always jealous when I get to see what kind of environment he gets to spend his day in. At the moment, for example, his classroom is set up as a kind of jungle. You have to climb through vines and leaves to get in – though if you are the

Year 1 student that they are intended for you can of course just walk underneath (otherwise I am sure there would be a Health and Safety issue about getting your jungle vines tangled around a neck or similar).

tip **If you go in during the holidays to sort out your room, it may be wise to take some of the following with you:**
Scissors Blu-Tack Staples/staple gun
Sellotape Staple remover
All schools have these, it's a matter of finding them!

Primary classrooms

Please note, key piece of advice coming up: **find out where the backing display paper is stored and take some now**! As far as I can ascertain, this is crucial in primary schools. Clearly the local LEAs need to take out shares in the companies that make this stuff, because schools get through reams of it. I'm pretty sure you could replenish the New Forest several times over with what the average primary school uses in a year – and yet, when it comes to grabbing some for yourself in September, you can bet that most of it will have gone already. Schools never seem to order enough in, so if you don't take it while it's there, you're going to be the one left waiting for the new delivery. This alone is a reason to decorate your classroom before the holidays really get under way.

Having discussed this with several experienced primary teachers, the following is a handy list of things that you can or should do in your room:

- Try to make something **individual** – make it stand out!
- **Link displays** to the work that you will be starting in September, e.g. for 'Castles and Dragons', set up a cardboard

castle: something that is interactive for the kids to actually go into or use. Later on in September you can ask the kids to bring in any toys that they have at home that may link to your work.

- Set up specific 'areas' in your room: **writing stations, make and do stations, science (discovery) stations, reading stations, imagination stations** and so on. You can also make and print 'sign-up' lists for these to monitor who has done what. It also helps the kids to feel involved in their learning.
- **Label everything**. This builds up independent learning as they find things on their own. Use word art on your PC and then laminate your labels – you can even add **photos** of what is inside the boxes, such as scissors. This is very helpful for younger children who can't read the words yet. It also looks very organised!
- Have on display copies of **reward systems and school rules**. You don't have to just type these up on a piece of A4 paper; you can make them eye-catching and place them somewhere that they can be referred to regularly. An example of a reward system would be weather pictures: a large sun/cloud, etc., and the kids' names printed out and laminated with Velcro to stick them with. This way, after bad behaviour they see their name move to a black cloud, but also see it move towards a sun when they improve. This links to **golden time** (or in this case, 'sunshine' time), so that if at the end of the week the students are on the sun, then they get to choose their own activities for the afternoon.
- **Assessment for Learning** bits and bobs are always a good idea. If you don't know what AfL is, look in Chapter 6. Depending on the age of your students guidance on how to improve work in kid-speak is always useful to refer to.
- **Bright and colourful** is the way to go for the beginning of the year – be experimental with borders! Get your hands on that backing paper and use adventurous lettering. You can order

things from websites, or schools may already have things like this in stock. They are easily ordered.

- Be as **imaginative as possible**: one teacher I know used to make huge structures using sheets that she had painted and plastic piping to make stuff like a space rocket to go in the corner of her room. These were almost like tents so the kids could go inside. This would obviously take some serious time on your part and you may well be under the impression that mucking about with piping and painting rocket exteriors on your best bedding is beyond the call of duty, but some people do enjoy these activities!
- Set up **an area outside your classroom**. An example could be a pirate ship or anything that links to the work you will be doing. This is really motivating for kids and can be used for role play and so on. It also creates great atmosphere and will make your classroom stand out from the rest.
- Do bear in mind that your room and furniture set-up will probably change continually throughout the year, so don't make anything too permanent. Make sure you can be **flexible**.

In general, you are aiming of course to make an impact from the start. The organisation of your room is going to reflect upon you as a teacher from the moment your kids step through the door in September. You want to draw them in immediately, and motivate them from the start. You will be seeing these students every school day from now until July – think carefully about what you want to do and how to do it. Then go for it!

It takes a lot of work but it's when other kids come into your room and say they wish they had a classroom like it that it all becomes worth it.

Secondary classrooms

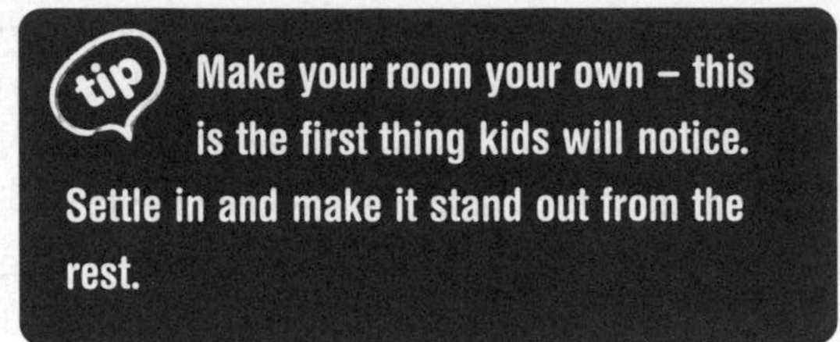

For some reason, there are secondary teachers who seem to think that display work is a bit beneath them. I've never quite understood this. For starters, any teacher in any key stage is surely so excited to finally have their **own room** – and to stop heaving enough bulky plastic boxes stuffed with books and lever arch files to cause Hulk Hogan to break out in a sweat – that they would be desperate to 'decorate' it and make it theirs to personalise their space.

Before I started at my new school last September, I went in on the first day of the summer holidays (admittedly not because I was keen, but so that I could then forget about it until September) and stuck up all my posters and so on that I had collected during the past four years. Now, as an RS, Ethics and Philosophy teacher, I have always found it crucial to make the most of my space to show the kids about the kind of lessons that they can expect and also a bit about what I am like as a teacher. I like images – lots of them – having been influenced by a couple of rooms that I saw in various schools in my PGCE year. I went into fabulous classrooms that were chock-a-bloc with amazing pictures, controversial eye-catching images, photographs that provoked thought and discussion just by their very existence, let alone by my referring to them in lessons. I plaster every available space with fantastic imagery, as well as level descriptors in kid-speak and a lot of Assessment for Learning bits and bobs and anything else that I can find that is a bit 'different'. I have always been desperate to veer as far away as possible from the dreaded stereotype of RS rooms, where you expect to get walloped about the head with a holy text as soon as you cross the threshold. So, if you are a secondary teacher, my advice would be that whatever your subject, make as much of your space as you can. Buy posters, make them and laminate things. Stick them everywhere! Print out key words and meanings; use as many references to pop culture as you can. I have had lots of comments in the past during parents' evenings from mums and dads who have been pleasantly surprised just to witness some vivid wall coverings in a secondary school, so rare is it in some to find anything worth looking at for long. As the year progresses, of course, you can also put up more and more of the students' work, which is always great for them to see.

Not only will all of this make you, your subject and your room seem a bit more interesting before you've even opened your mouth, it also creates a much more pleasant environment for you and the students to work in. **Make yourself at home**! At the risk of sounding as if I am about to do a turn as Whitney Houston and start gushing about how the 'children are our future', I'd also like to point out that this kind of environment can also help you – whatever your subject – to develop the spirituality of your kids. Because as all good teachers know, **any** subject on the curriculum should be doing this – despite the fact that many teachers dread hearing that word. Unfortunately, 'spirituality' did turn into a bit of a 'buzz word', which usually has the effect of diminishing the real importance behind a concept, but you should be just as likely to find spirituality in a maths or science classroom as you are in a music or an RS lesson – and it's good teachers who are utterly passionate about what they do that enable this to happen. Think back to Blake: cleanse those doors!

Before I move on to discuss the possibility of sharing classrooms, a word of caution and sympathy for those of us who are working in a school where even locks on doors do not prevent our rooms from being trashed the moment that we happen to step outside them – and sometimes even when we are still in them. This can at times be heartbreaking, not to mention demoralising and soul-destroying. It contributes to the many reasons why there are teachers who do not feel safe in their own classrooms, let alone the schools in which they work, and one teacher that I spoke to recently is currently battling away in just such a place. Unfortunately these are schools where the entire structure of discipline has broken down – in which case, try as you might as an NQT, you may be able to do nothing about it. All teachers need to be backed up with consistent sanctions and rewards and disciplinary systems – if you feel that these are not in place then you can either fight to help get them or you can brace yourself, get your head down, and after Christmas start scoping out the *TES* both online and in print. If you are dreading getting up in the morning, something is wrong. The great thing usually about teaching is that you know instantly whether it's the right profession for you – and you know instantly when something is amiss. If it is a comfort at all to you, the following tale is from an excellent teacher who happens to have ended up in a school where the SLT are failing both the staff and the kids and she has put up with months of relentless bad behaviour with no help from on high. **This is a rarity** – but for some teachers, it is a reality. She has taken matters into her own hands, and has no intention of staying on past the summer.

My classroom was broken into every day for a week, despite being locked. Every day my things were wrecked and the drawers of my desks turned inside out, with the contents being stolen. Eventually, after no help whatsoever from SLT, I emptied the desk, got pieces of A4 paper, wrote 'GET OUT!' on each of them, and filled the drawers. I am waiting to see what response I get.

So, this may not be the 'professional' way to deal with the issue, but it is the 'human' way – in the sense that this is a real example from a real teacher – and whilst it is by no means advice, it does sometimes help to hear that if you're struggling, you're not alone. If this is you, then seek help. Friends outside the school, the systems within the school, your union rep – speak to someone as soon as you can.

tip **If you teach a lesson in someone else's room, always leave it as you found it. Leaving a mess behind you is not professional and is a sure way to irritate colleagues.**

Advice on sharing classrooms

Generally, if you are a full-time teacher in a primary or secondary school, sharing a room is a rarity. If you are part-time or job-sharing, clearly you need to discuss the room with whoever you are sharing with. Secondary teachers who are part-time may move around the school all day, in which case it is both unnecessary and inappropriate to change or interfere with the room you are teaching in: this is because you will be 'borrowing' a room from someone else who is likely to be on a non-contact. This can be frustrating both for you and the person on the non-contact – we usually like to be able to get on with marking and planning and so on in the comfort of our own classroom, after all. Unfortunately, though, there is little that you can do about it other than to be respectful of the way in which the room is laid out by the person to whom it 'belongs'. There is nothing worse than coming back to your room and finding that furniture has been moved about or that there are still great volumes of writing on the board or mess everywhere.

If, however, you are part-time and based in the same room for several days a week – which may happen in primary or secondary teaching – then you can obviously have some say over the layout. It may be that you are in there for two days a week with the rest being taken up by 'floating' classes, particularly in a secondary environment. If this is the case, you can probably decorate it as you wish. If you are part-time in a primary school, the chances are that you are sharing a class and need to consult with the other teacher – but this should not pose a problem. It just means that you can both go about deciding what to put up and where. Share the responsibility between yourselves and go with the flow.

Classroom organisation

As I mentioned before, it is always lovely when you finally get your own room. Having spent years lugging stuff about, you now get to organise yourself and leave things where you want them, when you want to. Your room should already have some furniture in it, of course, but if you feel that you need extra storage, you can always check with your school as to whether further bookcases/shelving, etc. can be ordered. If all else fails, bring in bits yourself. It's terrible to admit, but very often teachers end up spending their own cash on things rather than go through the paperwork and effort of applying through the school. If it doesn't cost much, this isn't too bad – as long as you make sure it's something that you take with you should you ever move room or school – but don't get caught up in paying for too many things yourself. If you wanted to be in a job where you could easily afford to do this, let's face it, you wouldn't be in a classroom right now!

One thing you will notice as soon as you start the job 'for real' is that the amount of paperwork you will have to do will border on the ridiculous. I firmly believe that many teachers could easily make good use of a part-time PA, despite the fact that we are no longer supposed to get admin to slave over. You will need to organise pastoral versus academic paperwork, and it is often good to have a few lever arch files ready to help you. At some schools, the tutors are not based in their teaching rooms for tutor time; instead, they have to carry a huge folder of tutorial stuff about with them to morning and afternoon registration. For some people this is, unsurprisingly, a hassle. Staff are expected to be ready and waiting outside their rooms at the start of every lesson, prompt, to greet the students who line up outside. All very well if you've just had your tutor group in there, not so good if you're halfway across the school and the class you're late for are not the most settled and orderly of individuals. In the main, of course, this applies far more to secondary teachers, whereas those primary teachers among us seem to have the benefit of remaining in their beautifully set-out classrooms basking in the glory of their lovely wall displays. (Although my husband did recently return from lunch to find that one of his students had managed to obtain an illicit Pritt stick from somewhere and had randomly stuck pieces of paper to each available surface, including wall displays and desks. When questioned as to why she had done so, she replied meekly, 'I didn't feel well, Mr Howard'. I **love** primary school tales in comparison to secondary ones!)

So, before September comes, you can if you wish start to organise your room and set up a few items and some displays. However, if you'd rather leave that until you begin the term, then do bear in mind that you'll get some time if you have INSET, and also some time after school.

> **tip** **Organisation is key!**
> **If your department don't give you the following, buy your own –**
> **Filing trays** **Lever Arch Folders**
> **Subject Dividers** **Highlighters**
> **Tissues** **Biros** **Pencils**
> **(and it's always good to keep a few (nut-free) sweets on hand for rewards, though possibly not very PC!)**

To plan or not to plan

The level of planning that you do before September is, of course, entirely up to you. You may be the kind of person who feels reassured once organised, or you may prefer to leave things until you actually get in there. Either way you can guarantee that whatever you plan, it will probably still need to change at the last minute. Therefore, it can be just as wise to leave things as it can be to try and get a head start. Do whatever suits you, but remember it may turn out to be wasted time in the sense that you might not use the planning, – though it's never wasted if it keeps you happy for the time being.

The best thing you can do is ensure that you have a copy of your timetable before July – schools always have these ready by then. You can then see what is expected for the first week back. If you are lucky, you will be working in a school that has well-planned schemes of work (ask or email your HoD for these) and plenty of resources to accompany them, but either way it's best to get your own take on your classes and then begin planning accordingly. What works with some students in a class just won't work with others, and until you've met them you won't know. From this point of view, then, the advice is to relax. Do whatever makes you feel better in the meantime, but don't stress about it too much. Although when we first go into teaching we tend to think that the holidays are frequent and go on for ever, this doesn't last. Before long, you'll be on your knees begging for half-term – so make the most of the summer break!

Chapter 3

September: Part One

The greatest amount of change for you will be occurring during September, and subsequently this rather busy time of year is divided into two chapters. This chapter will be broken down into various sections. It is intended as a guide to your first couple of days or so in your new job and will include the following:

- INSET days – what to expect
- Beginning of term advice
- People you need to meet as soon as possible
- Organising yourself and being ready to meet the students; and
- Ideas for your class or tutor group

Generally this is groundwork stuff and is aimed at helping you to get settled and to know what you can expect from your first few days in the job. Specific ideas concerning lessons, planning and class management will be dealt with in the following chapter, September: Part Two.

Information you will need beforehand

> **tip** If you start back on an INSET day find out first if you need to wear 'work' clothes or not – the chances are it's jeans and casual clothing instead.

So here you are: the summer holidays fly by and suddenly it's your first day at your new school. All NQTs feel differently about their first days at work. Much can depend upon whether or not you have friends at the school or if you did a placement there. You may have been into work over the holidays and you may even have started there before July; if this is the case then you may not feel too nervous. Either way, the start of September is usually an exciting time and very often the most motivating time of year. Even if you are very nervous, the following example of a shameful INSET experience should cheer you up. This is actually my own tale. I am still embarrassed now by what might have been.

On my first INSET day in my new school I hadn't realised that it was OK to wear jeans and a T-shirt or anything casual. I wore instead black trousers and a long black jacket. Thankfully the jacket was thigh length and I hadn't removed it during the morning, because by the time I went to the loo at break I realised that the entire crotch seam of my trousers had split from front to back. My knickers would have been on display to all and sundry and I was absolutely mortified. To this day I am still thankful that a.) My jacket was long, and b.) The kids weren't in. I would never have lived it down. I still had to spend the rest of the day in a state of nerves, knowing that beneath my coat my trousers were flapping about my bottom and flashing my underwear.

A 'typical' INSET day

A typical school year begins with INSET days (or 'Incest Days' as some teachers jokingly call them). Secondary schools may have two of these at the start of each year, and sometimes primary schools will have none. Primary teachers tend to do much more in the way of summer preparation due to the need for displays and so on and are therefore thrown in at the deep end on the very first day back. Schools in general have five INSET days a year. Sometimes (in 2007/08, for example) something like a new secondary National Curriculum will be introduced for the following year and an extra INSET will be given in order to allow schools time to prepare. Your school may deal with these days by subsuming them in twilight sessions after work and therefore breaking up early by two or three days for Christmas, for example, but this is a contentious issue and opinions about them vary greatly among staff depending on their personal responsibilities outside work.

You will soon notice that the opinion of the general public is that teachers spend INSET days dallying about at home and perhaps indulging in a spot of marking should the fancy take them. Understandably these days may cause childcare issues for some parents, but then the education system is not a childcare service – and ultimately, INSET days and staff training are in the interests of the students, not the teachers. Of course, there are also many members of the general public who are fully supportive of teachers, and you will get a real buzz when some of these people make a huge effort to let you know how much they appreciate what you do for their kids. Nevertheless, a word of warning is necessary about public opinion and how to deal with it.

Of all aspects of teaching, INSET days seem to cause the most annoyance for the people who honestly believe that teachers clock off at 3 pm and swan off home to sit in the garden (although holidays are a source of equal irritation for them). This may sound negative, but at some point between now and next September you are likely to suffer a few jibes about your 'easy' life. In reality of course INSET days are usually taken up with training, meetings, briefings, preparations, SoW (Scheme of Work) reviews and hard work. They are not usually great fun, but they can be **very** useful indeed. It's often nice to see colleagues in a context where you can be more relaxed and less preoccupied by the usual pressures of the day. To begin the term with INSET days is always extremely beneficial. It gives you a chance to feel more organised and steady on your feet. You can meet and greet and get a feel for the staff in your year group or department, and you can touch up your classroom and sort your timetable. In short, they help you to feel prepared and a little more stable and secure in your new environment. You may find it very frustrating to hear these constant digs about INSET days, but the very reason this is frustrating is that most of us have enough work to do – on top of teaching actual lessons – to justify employing a part-time PA (and still have paperwork left over).

You may be in a primary school where your PPA is lost most weeks (check this out with a union if it does happen) or you may be in a secondary school where you teach five hundred kids a week. Either way you'll be swamped with teaching, planning, marking, paperwork, reports, meetings, parents' evenings, twilight sessions, afternoon clubs, options evenings and so on – so make the most of INSET. They don't give you much time, but without even this tiny allowance, the children of the people who criticise teachers would have a worse education because **we are not superhuman**. So take it on the chin and instead imagine the person who is being offensive standing in front of thirty disaffected students and trying to entertain and control them day in day out. This will invariably bring the smile back to your face.

INSET Day (or first day back) checklist

This is a list of key basics – do not overload yourself, just organise yourself

1 Ensure that you have received a diary or planner
2 Ensure that you have your timetable
3 Copy out key dates if you have not yet done so
4 Plan your week ahead and try to keep planning one week in advance
5 Find out the key people in school and the times for how the school runs (e.g. break, etc. but also staff briefings and so on)
6 Have a map of the school

More on these later...

A typical INSET day at the start of term will include the following. Obviously it will differ for primary and secondary in certain aspects, but it will involve more or less the same key elements.

Staff meeting

This may be one of the few full staff meetings you will attend this year if you're in a secondary school. Although there are frequent morning briefings, a full staff meeting is also very useful and far easier to organise at the start of the year when everyone is in the same place. In primary schools you may well have a full staff meeting once a week after school, but due to the sheer volume of staff working in a secondary school that may have two thousand students on roll, it is a far rarer event. Depending again on what age group you teach, you may also have to sit through a very detailed analysis of GCSE and A Level results. Any news over the summer holidays will be relayed and (sometimes embarrassingly) all new members of staff will be pointed

> **tip** Find out your system password asap and any computer programs that you need to use and how to use them (registers etc.).
> Ensure that you are provided with your laptop if you're supposed to have one (you almost certainly are).

out to the current staff members. You will have to wave and smile and so on, but the chances are that no one will even remember your name by the end of the meeting, so you can still sink into the background for a bit if you're the kind of person who likes to find their feet before making their mark.

Department meeting (more usual in secondary) or year group meeting (e.g. Year 2)

During this meeting you will be introduced (or reintroduced) to the members of your department and to the Head of Department, sometimes referred to as a Lead Practitioner. There may also be a Second in Department or you yourself may have either of these roles – it's by no means unheard of to land yourself a leadership position in your NQT year.

The likelihood is that results will be spoken about if appropriate, a motivational talk will be given, things will be handed out (more often than not a fair amount of paperwork) and expectations for the year ahead discussed. You should also have a copy of your timetable by now. Usually these meetings are light-hearted and everyone is in a good mood and ready to face the year ahead. It can be now that you begin to form true impressions of the school that you have chosen because these are the people you are going to be working with each day. It is wise to keep your head down for a while and suss them out and decide how best to approach each personality. A word of warning, odd as it may seem, is to **trust no one yet**! This is not meant in a conspiratorial way or written in order to disturb you – more a case of not making any brash comments or taking the mickey out of anyone that you have met so far and so on. People within schools are very closely linked and often married to one another or good friends – you don't want to offend your colleagues before you even teach your first lesson!

Lunch

A minor part of the day, but it can be a useful social tool. It is fairly normal on an INSET day for the school to provide lunch – you may need to check this before you go, but usually you'll have been posted a guide to the day already. You shouldn't need to take your own food, but you may need to 'sign up' to a meal beforehand.

This can actually be a daunting affair. It's a bit like one of those awful 'first date' meals where you don't want to stuff your face and nor do you wish to leave traces of your meal across it or in between your teeth. However, you should be treated to a pleasant lunch and a chance to get to know other people. This is good because it's informal – you can actually begin to socialise a bit and to chat about things that may have nothing to do with school. If you're new to the area as well, you can ask people questions about it and perhaps find out what is going on in the evening, places to visit and so on.

Year team meetings or pastoral meetings

For secondary teachers this involves getting to meet the other tutors in your year team as well as the Head of Year. This is always interesting because you get such a variety of year heads. A teacher at a school in the south of Hampshire had an interesting take on this:

I've worked for two HoY – one of whom was incredibly organised. She took no nonsense and despite the fact that the kids would moan about her, they did respect her. Her year group was by far the best behaved in the school. The other HoY was new to the job. He had more of a jokey relationship with the students and would let smaller misdemeanours go without really confronting the issues. The kids liked him but I felt that respect was missing –

they weren't overly well-behaved and some were allowed to slip through the net. There was an inconsistency and they did not know where their boundaries lay.

This is interesting because it just goes to show how much a Head of Year influences the students that are under their charge. Regular assemblies, regular contact, consistency and so on all make a huge difference – and you will be able to learn from observing your HoY over the course of September to July just how you would like to do it yourself should you wish to follow a pastoral route in education.

This particular meeting is crucial if you are a tutor (some schools don't give NQTs a tutor group, which is a shame in a way because it can be fantastic to have one) or even if you are only assigned to a year group, for example, if you are part-time. During the course of the meeting you should find out:

1. When **registers** are taken, how (e.g. laptop/paper), where they then go and so on;
2. Whether or not you will even be expected to take a register (in some schools the **legal register** is taken in periods 1 and 5);
3. Students who pose a **cause for concern**;
4. Who your **tutor group** are and a list of them, including their SEN etc.;
5. Methods for **contacting home** and so on if necessary;
6. When **assemblies** are held, who takes them, and where they are;
7. Whether or not you will have your **tutor base** in your own teaching room or elsewhere;
8. **Sanctions and rewards** (going on report etc. and how to put a student on report). This can be interesting because one school I know of actually has different systems across the year groups – which lacks consistency and is not overly successful;
9. What **activities** happen in tutor time (quizzes, silent reading and so on);

10 What to do if you suspect a child has a **problem** (there will be more on this later);
11 What is done to accommodate **PSHE** (often nothing to do with the year team but sometimes as a tutor you will have to teach it);
12 You may also be given **homework diaries** to hand out and other **information**.

If you are in a primary school your 'year team' will generally include yourself and two or three other teachers, though this will depend on how large the school is and how it is structured. The huge difference here, of course, is that you will have your class each day every day, not just a tutor group who you clap eyes on twice daily, sometimes less than that when taking assemblies into account. Instead, you will have the benefit of **really** getting to know these kids. Hopefully they'll be lovely, and if not, there is advice later in the book on how you can help them to become a little closer to lovely. Either way, you are going to have an extremely close relationship with these children and also their parents. In secondary school, teachers see much less of the vast majority of parents. Rare is the day that students are picked up from school, for example, whereas you are likely to see mums or dads twice a day. If you are with a very young year group, you may well have to lead them out on to the playground or a similar area at the end of the day. They will meet their parents or carers there and so will you. You will have far more responsibility for their safety as they leave school (e.g. ensuring that they are collected) and all this can be discussed with the team you work in.

Remember also if you are a primary teacher that (unless you are with Year R) you can be given a very detailed handover from the class's previous teacher. This can include not only pastoral issues but also information on behaviour and learning styles. Do not be afraid to ask other teachers if there is anything that you feel you need to know. You should **never base your opinion solely on someone else's** – we all know that **different kids are different**

with different teachers – but it can help to be forewarned (or forearmed with plenty of strategies).

New staff meeting

More often than not there will be a meeting for all new staff. Ideally this will include the Head, but if not then the person in charge of new staff induction should be present. This is a fantastic opportunity to meet other NQTs: the likelihood is that you'll attend various meetings with them throughout the year and will be supportive of each other. There may be no other NQTs at the school for this year, but even in a place with a very low staff turnover you're bound to meet other new people. Some of these may not even be on the teaching staff, but they will at least be 'newbies' like yourself! This will probably be a very brief meeting – which is a good thing as you'll have a few more to get through before your (very long) day ends.

Duty team meeting

This is very important in a secondary school due to the sheer size of the place and the number of staff and students, and it is very important in a primary school due to the age and vulnerability of some of the students.

Depending on your school structure there are usually several Duty Team Leaders. This may be a Head of Year or a Head of Department. The best schools take duty very seriously – it's a pain in the backside, but the kids would run amok without it. You won't usually be called upon to do a lunch duty, but if you are you should actually **get paid** for it – so you may wish to offer your services.

Duties are usually before school begins, during break times, and after school. You should only have to do two of these sessions and normally on one day of the week only. Your DTL will wander around the grounds and ensure that you're out and about in your designated area and that you're OK – and do remember gloves and a brolly in the winter months. Duty is a good opportunity to get to know some of the kids, but it can be daunting too. Check during your meeting as to what the policy is for confrontations in the playground etc. and who to call. It's hard enough when you know a student's name sometimes – but when you're clueless as to who a person is, you can feel powerless.

When on duty, try to chat to as many kids as possible. This will enhance your reputation around the place and also give you a chance to learn names. It helps the students to realise that you are a human being and that there is not meant to be a power struggle going on between staff and students – break down any kind of 'us and them' situation. We're all in the education system together and should all be working together. Unfortunately, for various reasons, some schools do not succeed in creating this ethos within their environment and instead it can become very much a 'battle', with staff on one side and students on the other. This is never productive and only ever detrimental. But remember: whatever the school is like, **you are still an individual within that establishment**. Let the students see that your attitude is one of mutual respect and they will begin to appreciate that and work with you, not against you.

Something that is interesting to note in different schools is how often the SLT are seen out and about. This can vary a great deal and makes a vast impact on the school. In one school that I taught in I remember being astonished when I asked a variety of pupils to drop something into the Head's office for me – none of them had any idea where it was, and they were in Year 9! In another school, the staff commented that it was very rare to actually see the Head out and about patrolling corridors and so on. This was in stark contrast to a teacher elsewhere who said that the Head was seen on a daily basis, known by everyone, consistently out in the playground as well as in the buildings, and working on a rota with other members of the SLT. It is not difficult to guess which school had the better behaviour and excellent working relationships with mutual respect between staff and pupils.

Performance Management reviews

Whoever said that this was an exercise in box-ticking? Hmmm, I'll leave it up to you and your judgement, once you've completed your first year, to decide.

It may sound odd when you consider that you are only just starting out, but these will be done near the **beginning** of the academic year. The usefulness of the exercise depends on the school you're in: some places fill these out and they are never looked at again until the following September, when the previous year's form will be dragged out (if it can be found) and your objectives ticked off. The key, of course, is to set targets that you can achieve – but you do need to take a lot of care here to ensure that you are **not taken advantage of**. This is very important to you as an NQT and bears mentioning in more detail.

Your performance management review will usually take place each September. It will be held by your line manager. In some schools it will then be reviewed in January, or thereabouts, in an Interim Performance Management Review, before being completed the following September. Generally around three targets are set, and one of these is usually a statistic, linked to exam or level results.

An example of a pro forma for Performance Management:

THE EXAMPLE SCHOOL

Performance management: initial meeting

Member of Staff: A. Teacher

Job Title: Classroom teacher Start Date: Sept 2008

Main Responsibilities: Tutor group and general classroom teacher responsibilities

Date covered by this review: from 1 September 2008 to 31 August 2009

Date of initial meeting: 1 Sept 2008

Objectives agreed:

	Objectives	Success criteria and evidence
1	Student progress Students in GCSE class to achieve 75% A* – C pass rate	Measured on summer 2009 results Residuals to be considered
2	Professional practice Develop use of ICT and e-learning with Virtual Learning Environment	Produce SoW that are updated to include Year 7 use of laptops for 50% of lessons
3	Career development Gain experience of leadership within the department in order to enhance career profile	Shadow HoD Attend course on leadership and middle management Produce set of aims for the department to follow in one key area (e.g. e-learning)

Moderated by Head teacher: Signature: ______________________

Signed: ________________ Reviewer ______________ Date

This review concludes in the reviewer making a recommendation:

Reviewee's progression to UPS: (Y/N)

Date of interim meeting: (Y/N)

Performance management: Teacher monitoring and interim meeting

NOTES

Member of staff:

Date covered by the review: from to

Date of this meeting

OBJECTIVE 1

Notes from discussion

On target? Yes/No

Targets needed for completion

OBJECTIVE 2

Notes from discussion

On target? YES/NO

Targets needed for completion

OBJECTIVE 3

Notes from discussion

On target? YES/NO

Targets needed for completion

Signed: ______________ Reviewee ______________ Date

Signed: ______________ Reviewer ______________ Date

Performance management: review meeting

Member of staff:

Job title:

Date covered by this review: from to

Date of this meeting:

Outcome of objectives | Evidence provided? Achieved? (Y/N)

1		
2		
3		

Assessment of overall performance

Where eligible for UPS progression – is progression recommended? Y/N ☐

Signed: ____________ Reviewee ____________ Date

Signed: ____________ Reviewer ____________ Date

The interim sheets and review meeting are then held mid-year and end of year respectively. Some schools may have very detailed forms (this one is pretty detailed) and others may have something far more basic, with no need for an interim report.

The examples on this form are fairly basic. You may be asked to go into far more detail and – sometimes – as an NQT you may be asked to do far too much. This is something you need to watch out for. The vast majority of schools do not take advantage of their NQTs (in fact you should essentially be fairly 'protected' for your first year), but some do. There will be more information later about knowing your rights and asserting them, but in terms of your workload and your line manager's expectations of you, you should be prepared to draw the line if you feel it necessary. An example from a teacher I have spoken to in a secondary school illustrates this:

I'm currently a GTP student but have been offered a job here at the school to start in September. I agreed to take the position and was pleased that I could complete my NQT year in an environment with which I am now familiar. However, it has become increasingly apparent as July approaches that I'll have to look out for myself during the next year. Various jobs – usually the ones that no one else wants to do – seem to be heading my way. Uploading past exam papers onto the website, doing **all** of the display boards for the faculty that I'm in, typing up SoW and uploading them and so on. I've been used to cover tutor groups already this term – something that students are not supposed to do – but now I feel a line is being crossed. It inspires no loyalty in me – I want to complete my NQT year and leave.

A fairly obvious problem here is the fact that secondary school teachers are no longer supposed to do display work. In terms of decorating your classroom it is clearly up to you how much work and effort you put in – after all, this benefits you directly and the learning of your students. However, if someone asks you to do the display boards around the school – which can take **hours** – you should try to be assertive. In many schools there will a person who is specifically employed to do displays as part of their job description. The boards that one often sees in reception areas and so on may be designed by this person and they will be changed on a rotational basis so that different departments throughout the year

> **tip** **Don't be afraid to keep asking questions about who is who and where things are – people are usually more than willing to help.**

can show off their work. There may be 'Work of Excellence' displays – but again, although it may be your responsibility to choose the work, it is not your responsibility to display it. This is easier said than done, but if you feel that you are being taken advantage of, do try to speak up. Your mentor is usually the person to speak to.

After your review is completed (and this may not happen at the start of term as some schools leave it until after half-term) this will usually be the end of your first full day in the school.

> **tip** Sometimes you build yourself up so much for one day and feel such relief at getting through it that you end up a bit depressed afterwards at the thought that you need to do it again the next day – just try to take one day at a time. Ease yourself into the term and don't burn yourself out.

You survived – congratulations!

People you need to meet as soon as possible

During your first days at your new school, there are people who you are going to need to introduce yourself to as soon as possible. Hopefully your mentor will think of this already, but do put yourself out and go to the trouble of finding the people in question. We all feel like pests sometimes in new environments, constantly asking questions and needing to check directions and so

> **tip** You should certainly have met the SLT by now so I won't include them here – if you haven't, ask to be introduced or at least have them pointed out to you.

on, but this is how you'll get to know your new workplace. Assuming that by now you have met all of those with whom you'll be working in close proximity, the following list will give some idea of the other staff members that you need to see to make settling in that little bit easier.

New staff 'buddy'

Many schools now provide new staff with a 'buddy'. This can be a great system because you'll meet the person (usually someone who was recently a new member of staff themself, or at least someone that the school know to be very friendly and willing to help), and then if you need advice, you can ask them. On the other hand you may not even see them again for the rest of the academic year because you could settle in so quickly and seamlessly. Either way, it is a good indicator that the school place an emphasis on welcoming and supporting NQTs and other people who are new to the workplace.

Child Protection Liaison Officer (CPLO)

This is the person who deals with all issues of child protection. You as classroom teacher or tutor may be a first lookout for any problems, but the CPLO is the member of staff to whom any real concerns for child safety and so on will be passed. During your training year you were probably (hopefully) introduced to the CPLO at your placement schools. For some reason, trainees and NQTs are often the teachers to whom students will make a disclosure because in many ways they seem more approachable than the members of staff the kids have been surrounded by for years. If a child does ever wish to disclose information to you, you must make it clear that you **cannot and will not promise to keep anything confidential**. Our duty as teachers is to protect the students in our care and you will often be their first port of call – or the person to whom their friends may turn if they are concerned that there is an issue that is arising outside of the classroom. If you do hear of anything that is disturbing or worrying, pass it on immediately to the CPLO, who can begin to take the appropriate measures necessary.

websites

Union Web addresses:

NASUWT – **www.teachersunion.org.uk**

NUT – **www.teachers.org.uk**

ATL – **www.askatl.org.uk**

NATFHE – **www.natfhe.org.uk**

NAHT – **www.naht.org.uk**

Your union representative

This is important! It is more than likely that you will already belong to a union because you will be advised to join one in your training period, but if you do not, join one now! There are various unions to choose from, some of which are associated, for example, with more strike action than others (although the recent 2008 strike action over pay was the first in many years) and some that are aimed at Head Teachers alone. However, the two most common unions that are usually joined are the NUT (an acronym that causes much mirth among teachers and non-teachers alike) and the NASUWT. This doesn't mean that you have to belong to either of these, of course, and you may wish to research the others further now that you actually have to start paying for membership each month – but do make sure that you join a union. You may never seek its guidance, but teaching is a profession that can be perilous for various reasons, not the least of which is the very nature of the people we teach. Here is an example of a girl who had a frightening encounter on her first ever teaching placement:

I walked from the school to the local pub one evening to grab some food and saw two Year 11 boys. One of them commented that he had seen me at the bus stop in the mornings, so I smiled and went to order my meal. He said that he lived near the bus stop and why didn't

I pop into his place after school on the way home one day. I tried to laugh this off, unsure of how to react, and said that I didn't think that would be appropriate. He then insinuated that he would tell people I had, even if I didn't. I was terrified! I went to school the next morning and reported the incident to my Head. It was a situation that had to be nipped in the bud and it made me think of how important it is to ensure you are represented by a union, because you never know what kind of allegations might be made about you and when you'll need their support.

This is good advice with a good example to back it up. It pays to know who your union rep is in school and to attend the meetings they will usually hold to discuss local and national issues that arise throughout the year. Often your union rep will introduce themselves to you anyway and you'll find material from them in your pigeonhole from time to time. This is also the person that you can ask to come with you should you ever be called in to speak to the Head regarding a disciplinary matter and so on. If you are ever asked to go in and speak to the Head, do ask why this is: usually you'll be told why in advance and normally it's for informal chats about career progression or how you are finding the school. In fact, you may never have to go and speak to the Head in your NQT year (except for your lesson observation that they will carry out at some point – more on that later!).

You may of course find yourself in a school that does not have a representative of your particular union. This is unusual, and in fact some teachers with experience of this have commented on the difference they noticed between schools who do have a good rep in place and those that don't. An NQT who had recently moved to a new area within the United Kingdom had a story that clearly illustrates why it can be very useful to have a union rep on hand:

'I had recently been signed off sick and was very poorly but had put my name down some time before to go on a residential visit to an American state. This was taking place over the weekend and I went into work on the day before we were due to go. Various members of staff commented on the fact that I still looked and sounded so poorly – I could barely stand – but I couldn't let the kids down at such a late stage and knew that the school would have great difficulty in finding another teacher to go in my place, especially with it being abroad. In the end I still went and managed to keep my spirits up during the day with the students and gave them my all – and in the evenings, I just went to bed and rested. This was particularly exhausting as we had to be back in school the day after we returned to the UK.

A few days later I saw the Head who asked me to go and meet with her later that afternoon. I didn't think to ask why – and as there is no union rep at my school I didn't consider asking anyone to come in with me. When I met with the Head later that day I was astonished to find myself being told that she was disappointed with reports about my 'performance' on the trip. Apparently I gave the impression in school of being 'vivacious and up for it', but that she was told I was quiet and miserable during the evenings and not at all fun to be around! This was topped off by my being informed that she therefore believed I was not an appropriate member of staff to go on residential trips in the future. I was horrified and furious! There was no-one there to witness what she was saying and no-one who could advise me about the unprofessional comments she had made. I spoke to my friends and HoD but of course they couldn't do anything, although they were equally shocked.'

This of course is likely to be a rare example of being 'disciplined' and of inappropriate and unprofessional comments and behaviour. It is unlikely that the matter would have been dealt with in this way had a union rep been present – in fact, most Heads would not even see this as a 'matter' to start with! However, it does give a great example of a situation during which a union rep can be present. Generally you'd be told in advance if you were going to 'disciplined' in any way, shape or form, and the majority of teachers go through their careers with no need whatsoever for such measures. It's good to know, though, that you've got support if this does happen to you – and if there's no rep at your school, contact your local union office as they can advise you and send someone along.

tip **Be nice to *everyone*! By being bright and friendly and courteous and polite at all times to the admin staff you are going to make your life a lot easier. These are the people who hold the school together and get little credit for it – make them feel appreciated because you'll be amazed at how often you'll need them.**

The reprographics department

The person who does the photocopying in the school may seem at first like an odd choice of staff member to place on the list of those you must meet – but this is one of the people who will make your life easier, so get to know them now! In fact, you will invariably find yourself desperate at times to get stuff copied at the very last minute or even during a lesson, so make friends as soon as you can because you'll be seeing an awful lot of this person and they will be your lifeline to resources. Find out:

1 How to **use the machines** yourself, which machines you are allowed to use yourself, and what your personal or department code is.
2 How to place an '**order**': is there a slip you need to fill in and attach? What information do you need to put on there?

3 How much **notice** you need to give: four hundred laminated copies of a colour print are unlikely to get done any time soon. Plan in advance. It is highly frustrating to get stuck behind someone who is making several hundred copies of a resource if you only have five minutes of non-contact time left.
4 **How many copies** are you actually allowed to make across the year? There is a budget for these things.
5 Does the school have very basic (dare I say archaic?) **equipment**, e.g just a black-and-white copier, or is it a little more high tech than that? What can you actually do? Some schools are fantastic and you can make and create amazing resources and posters and so on. Others will copy sheets in black and white and that's it. Make sure you at least get decent copies – or use a printer instead, depending on who is paying for the cartridges.
6 Do not break **copyright law**! Usually there will be a reminder about this within a hair's breadth of the machine and often some instructions on operating it.
7 Work out carefully how many copies you need. **Recycle** those you never use.
8 Be careful about copying Over Head Transparencies (**OHTs**): some copiers go into meltdown unless you specifically input what you are doing and 'tell' the machine it's an OHT.

Be lovely to the person who is in charge of photocopying: they will be your friend! If you work in a school where there is no one to help with photocopying, then it doesn't take a lot to teach yourself but you will need to be organised.

tip At some point find out who the SENCO is – you will need their help for your SEN students and to find out about LSAs or TAs. Many schools have an excellent EAL department so investigate this as well if you have students with English as a foreign language.

The librarians (and using the library)

Most schools now have decent libraries – or so we hope – even in the age of the internet. Often the library will also have some laptops or PCs available to the kids and you will be able to book whole lessons in there. It is therefore important to find out how to go about doing this and who is going to help you – namely, the librarian/s. Some may think it odd to include the librarians in the list of people you should meet, but this just goes to show how undervalued they can be within the school system.

The vast majority of school librarians take their jobs very seriously, and rightly so: the library is a fantastic resource, and apart from the obvious options of reading and taking books out, the students need to know how to research. Some schools have very exciting systems like fingerprint swiping, so you may need to go and get your digits swiped as soon as possible in order to be able to take books out yourself. You may even be able to ask the librarian to put aside 'book boxes' for you that you can take to your class or tutor group for them to use. One school I trained in had an amazing library, complete with seminar room and IT rooms attached, and you could book these separately. As a trainee I really made the most of that library – it was pretty devastating for all involved when near to the end of the summer term the roof collapsed on it due to a burst sewage pipe and deposited the contents of the girls' and boys' toilets on to the resources, the computers and the books, not to mention the heads of the attending librarians. It was through sheer luck that I wasn't in there at the time, and through sheer strength of will that I kept my warped sense of humour controlled when we were told about the situation in assembly the next day. The vision of a poo swinging, suspended in the air by a ceiling rafter, stays with me still.

Library staff (when not covered in raw sewage) are usually very willing to help you but do ensure that you keep control of any students you have down there and that they treat the place with respect and are tidy and courteous. It's worth making a trip down to the library and introducing yourself. Familiarise yourself with the surroundings and what's available.

The IT department or technicians

tip One hurdle that I've found over the years is that either your own immaturity does not disappear the second you leave school yourself, or it's somehow reactivated by being around the kids. Best of all we expect them to control theirs whilst occasionally bursting with silent mirth ourselves. You will need to practise your best poker face for when situations such as the Poo in the Library occur – or rather, for when you are meant to look stern in assembly. The kids themselves appreciate nothing more in teachers than a good sense of humour.

Due to the fact that we now teach in an age where we use laptops, interactive whiteboards, VLEs and so on, it is important to find the IT department or technicians because if (when) something goes wrong with any of these pieces of equipment, they will be able to help you. Some schools now run everything on one network, including registration systems and so on, which can be a real pain when it all collapses – indeed, it can feel as though your entire day has gone down the pan. This does of course lend weight to the suggestion that it is best to ensure that all your lessons are backed up with old-fashioned paper resources and plans, especially in a primary school, where very often outside help needs to be called in to fix any problems. My current school recently held a conference where the Lead Practitioner for E-Learning was meant to give a presentation that involved using a virtual world that has been set up online for kids. He planned to show the assorted head teachers and other visitors just what was possible using technology. Alas, just as he joked that the system probably wouldn't work at all, the projector petered out, the technology failed and he just had to describe it instead. This is where a cry for help to the tech guys is needed, so find out where they are and befriend them immediately!

tip A 'VLE' is a Virtual Learning Environment – and most schools will now have one or will be in the process of setting one up. You will be trained on how to get the best out of the VLE and you will be expected to contribute to it. It's a bit like having a web page – you can do things like set up forums for your classes or get them to do blogs or wikis. Check with your mentor or HoD.

Many secondary schools now are trialling Year 7 laptop schemes. Each student in Year 7 will have a laptop for which their parents pay, for example, £5 a week. These payments continue until Year 9, when the laptop becomes their property. An issue here of course is those whose parents cannot afford to spend an extra £20 a month per child or who do not wish to. In this case, schools generally have some kind of 'bank' of spare laptops that teachers can book out for those students who do not have their own. SoW are supposed to incorporate a certain percentage of laptop use and departments must ensure that the technology actually enhances learning more than if the students did not have it. Therefore using the laptop as a word processor is not good enough: you need to be savvy with whatever VLE systems or similar the school has in place (Moodle and Sharepoint are examples). You may take issue here with the implications for handwriting and literacy, but whatever your own view you need to really know what you're doing if you'll be expected not only to teach your own subject but to also be relatively au fait with several IT systems. These are generally very easy skills to pick up and can make lessons very engaging. Training should be provided and it should be ongoing – if it is not sufficient, then don't be afraid to ask. You've been employed to teach and you should be given the opportunity to do so to the best of your ability.

A first-day checklist

> **tip** Chances are you'll have already met your class or tutor group during a day in June/July that the school invited you to, like an induction. In this case, you may feel a little more prepared.

Somewhere, in amongst all of this, the school will of course actually open up to the kids. Whether you have INSETs first or not, eventually there will be children in the place at some point during this week and you will be able to begin to do what you were employed for. In a secondary school you may find that you get another few days that are relatively quiet. Very often Year 7 will be back a day before anyone else, although Year 11 may also arrive on this day. Depending, then, on your timetable you may still not have to teach just yet. If you don't, then thank your lucky stars and use the time to prepare. If you do, or if you are a primary teacher, then it's full steam ahead from now until October half-term. The following are the main issues for your first few teaching days. After the first week or two you'll find yourself in a sudden rhythm and everything will become clearer. So, first of all, a basic checklist:

The top ten things to have at the ready:

1 Have a list at hand of your class or tutor group.

2 Make sure you know when the first assemblies are and what information you must give to your class or tutor group.

3. Ensure that you know your timetable and what you need to teach and where you are teaching.
4. Have your diary up to date by now with important dates and warnings written in ahead of time for things like reports and so on.
5. Find out about and be confident with registration systems.
6. Have your first week planned.
7. Know what the school's sanctions and rewards system is and be prepared to use it immediately.
8. Know how the technology in your room works.
9. Know where any equipment is that you need to give the students.
10. Know who to call if you need to call anyone and how to do so – often there will be a telephone system, so find out where the phones are. (There should also be a list of extension numbers next to it.)

Now, this may seem like a lot to do but it really is a **basic** checklist. Your room by now should be sorted out, whether you did it in the hols or you've been staying after school, and you should have been given your share of stationery and so on by another member in your year team or by your HoD if you are in a secondary school. During the meetings at the start of term or on the INSET day you will have been given information regarding start-of-term arrangements with the kids, so make sure you have them to hand – this will detail whether or not they have assemblies that you need to be at and take them to and so on, and you'll have to be ultra-prepared and organised.

Aside from that (as if it wasn't enough), let's have a look at some of the basics in a little more detail.

Your class or tutor group

This can be very exciting as well as nerve racking: these are the students that you will encounter more than any others as you'll be seeing them on a regular basis. **Very** regular if you are a primary teacher!

Whether you have had to go elsewhere in the school to greet them or whether they have come straight to your room, there will be a moment very soon when you will have to introduce yourself for the first time. Over the page are some ideas on how to begin building a relationship with them.

Information for your class or tutor group

Generally on a first day back there is a lot of admin to get through. It will help you to have a folder (a big one) to collate this info and collect pastoral information in. You will usually have been given a vast amount of paperwork already (not so much to pass on, of course, if you are teaching very young children) and will need to ensure that you're giving things out on time and getting them back in. For this reason it can help to have several **class lists** printed in advance, even if your registers are on your laptop. This way, you will be able to tick off who has been given what and who has handed what back in. Undoubtedly you'll then need to pass these bits on to other people, and various kids will have missed the deadline. Cover your back by being organised from the start because before you know it they'll be telling you that you didn't hand it out in the first place – and you'll be so tired that **you'll believe them**!

In a secondary school in particular you are very likely to have been handed a great pile of **homework diaries** to give out – and as tutor you may well need to sign these once a week and ensure that parents have done so too. Keep up to date with this: believe it or not, some parents do actually complain to schools that their

Try to build a real sense of group pride – pay close attention to uniform etc and encourage them to be to be smart. Let them know you're proud of them.

Some schools have merit-point systems. If so, stick a chart up totalling each student's achievements. If not, make up your own reward system instead.

Build their self-esteem

Settle the kids in your usual teaching style, introduce yourself and sound really positive about how excited you are to be their teacher or tutor. Set your high expectations immediately and don't back down from them.

Make quizzes for them as a part of the weekly routine. Some year groups have inter-class or tutor competitions. Motivate them.

Deal with behaviour just as you would with any class. Make the ground rules clear.

With new classes in some year groups certain games can be used – the kind of 'bonding' ones that adults loathe but kids like – to get to know each other. EG: sit in a circle and tell the person next to you your name and a fact about yourself. Go round the circle with your partner introducing yourself, and so on.

Have a laminated copy of the school rules and mottoes up on the wall, as well as uniform regulations. Refer to them when needed – you are their key daily contact and can have quite an impact.

Take photos of the kids (bear in mind that some schools have policies on this) to stick on a board in your room – give them a sense of ownership of it and pride in their group or class.

child's diary has not been signed frequently enough. You'd also do well to advise them against scrawling graffiti over their diaries. This won't have much of an impact for very long, but it may help them to look reasonably smart and organised until mid-September at least. (Although, bless them, there are always a few girls who love stationery so much that they will keep theirs pristine with a little bookmark tucked inside it right up until July. Without being sexist at all, merely observational, I am yet to see a boy who does so.)

This is probably also a good time to mention **Collective Worship**. This may be dealt with via assemblies but some schools do give out booklets with 'Thoughts for the Day' or similar contained within. You will be required to read these out to your class or tutor group. If you work in a primary school, you may get away with doing so; if you work in a secondary school and have Year 8 or above, the chances are you'll get sniggered at or laughed away from the front of the classroom. For some reason, these 'Thoughts' are nearly always unspeakably naff. You may actually be able to come up with your own instead – because it is a fact that school should enhance children's spirituality. This need have nothing whatsoever to do with religion. Instead it should be about getting them to consider the bigger picture in life and what their life means to them and to others. You can therefore enhance spirituality through speaking about football if you so wish – and you'd get a far better response than if you read out a prosaic piece of text about helping others. Crucial as this may be in life, it doesn't alter the fact that the kids have heard it all before. They'll be far more inspired by something that is relevant to them, rather than something that turns them off completely.

Assemblies are nearly always held for at least one year group on the first day of term, or for the whole school if you are in a smaller establishment. Make sure you know where you are going. In a primary school these first assemblies will usually be held by the Head but in secondary it is often the responsibility of the Year Head or SLT if it's Year 11/12/13 and some motivation is needed to get the exam year started.

Sometimes you will get members of staff who hold outstanding assemblies and seem to have a natural gift for it. At other times you will have to cringe for some poor soul who clearly isn't comfortable with the idea at all. Funnily enough, just because we all stand up in front of classes and speak to them, there is something quite different about standing up in front of a hall of kids and other members of staff. I loathe the idea of doing an assembly, and you may too – depending on the school you're in, though, you may at some point have to hold one. Often you can get your class to do it, and at other times you may quite like the idea of showing off a bit yourself (isn't that partly what teaching is all about?), but I am in true admiration of the teacher from the following tale:

In my last school a member of SLT was supposed to be holding the assembly. Usually he was very good at doing so and would generally start by playing bands such as The Killers and getting the kids feeling quite motivated and alert. On this particular day though, we all waited and waited and he just didn't show up. None of us ever found out why he didn't, but in the end a female teacher took matters into her own hands and just stood up and started speaking about the concept of 'fear'. She told the kids about her recent holiday to Florida and how she had held a tarantula and a snake for the first time, and had managed to conquer her fear by facing it head on. Fantastic stuff! We all applauded madly at the end because none of us had been brave enough to do it and she showed real initiative – not to mention captivating the kids.

In secondary school the students will generally have two assemblies a week: usually a year group one and an SLT one. Often these will be in different areas of the school, so do make sure you know your way around a little and that you have passed the info on to your tutees. Assemblies may be morning or afternoon depending on where you teach, and you will often need to take a register there. If this is difficult at first because you don't know their names, just ask the students to stay behind at the end and call a register. Alternatively, get a reliable member of the class to go through the register with you and let you know who is there. Bearing in mind that it is a legal document, it may be best to stick with the former option until you get to know the students a little better.

Timetables are also something that you may need to give out (though many secondary schools will have done so in July). The kids will invariably have lost these, though, and changes will have been made. Hand them out and get the students to stick them into their diaries or put them somewhere relatively safe. If you have new students you may even have maps to give them – or the school may have been sensible enough to have one printed in the diaries. This is useful for you too: swipe a map if you can!

Generally, once you've done the basics with your class or tutor group you can either send them off to lessons (often this first tutorial of the year may last as long as two hours) or begin to teach them if you are in primary school. This then leaves you ready to start teaching yourself and possibly meeting your classes for the first time – nerve-racking but exciting!

tip **For these first few weeks you may feel as if you are in a daze and rushed off your feet. This will pass as you get into the rhythm of the term.**

Beginning to teach

Clearly this is crucial, and since the term began it is probably one of the things that you have dwelt on the most. Hopefully, then, you are prepared, in lesson terms at least, to get going. You should know exactly what you are up to for these first few lessons and should have planning and resources coming out of your ears. If you are in a primary school, you should know what your year group are covering and will be with your class already, and if you are in a secondary school, you should aim to be at the door of the room you are teaching in (hopefully but not always your own) ready to greet the students and set a tone of discipline for the lesson.

As soon as you begin the lesson, do ensure that you start as you mean to go on. Keep an order and routine. Begin with the **register** (this is actually a policy in many schools) and introduce yourself and your expectations. This will be much the same as to what you'll have done with new classes during training, and you may already have a technique for getting to know names and so on. If your school requires that you register each class or session on a laptop, then make sure you know how to use the system and that you also know what to do if the system fails and you need to report the info via old-fashioned pen and paper.

Make sure you have **exercise books** ready to give out and that you know where these will be kept between lessons. Some teachers prefer the students to take them, depending on space, while others prefer to have specific areas in their rooms for book storage and do not allow the kids to wander off with them except if they are necessary for homework tasks. You may even need to register their **homework** tasks on a system such as Class Server and the school may set this out in a policy. If so, keep up to date with it at the end of each lesson. Tempting as it is to load it all online at the start of each week, tasks usually differ as the week goes along and you may be further ahead (or behind) than you thought you'd be.

If you intend to teach using PowerPoint or your interactive whiteboard immediately, then make sure that everything is up and running before you get going and that the **technology** is working. Also have a back-up plan and make your lessons as engaging as possible to begin with – go in with a bang and make a great impression. (There will be more on actual **lessons and planning** in the following chapter if you wish to scoot ahead and have a look.)

There is every chance that you will have to use either a **sanction** or lots of **rewards** in your first few lessons. You need to make sure that you know what the school policies are. If, for example, you need to fill out Cause for Concern forms, then have some ready in your desk or a folder. There will also be ideas for **discipline and class management** in the following chapter, with various ideas for each as well as ideas for rewards. For now, though, just make sure that you know who to call if you need to and how to go about doing so.

A final note here really is just to say that you've actually been doing this for quite some time already: you **are** a teacher with many skills, and in your NQT year you now begin the process of honing those skills. It's funny, because no matter how good a student teacher you may have been, you will invariably end up looking back at the end of your NQT year and being **amazed** at how far you've come. Have confidence in your abilities now and look ahead to the new academic year for what it is: an opportunity to be the best you can be. Grab the chance and make the most of it. Believe it or not, it won't be long before you're starting your second year and meeting those new classes all over again.

Chapter 4

September: Part Two

This chapter is designed to help you get to grips with the real basics of teaching and to give very practical ideas that you can carry straight over into your own classroom:

- Relationships with the students
- Your first lessons
- Learning names
- Class management
- Rewards and sanctions
- Captivating lesson activity ideas

September is always one of the busiest times in the school year and very often feels like a mad rush until you have settled into your new routines. It's always nice to complete the first week with your class or classes. If you are in a primary school you'll probably have sussed out a few of your pupils by now, and if you are in a secondary school you'll have met all your classes at least once and will know what to expect from them. Also, of course, they will now have some idea of what to expect from **you** – which leads us to the tricky subject of whether or not you need to worry about being liked or loathed and upon which factors this depends. In the end, your most important relationship in school is going to be the one with the students and everything else rests upon this foundation, so let's start there.

> ***websites***
>
> If you haven't done so already check out –
>
> **www.ratemyteacher.com**
>
> Brace yourself! The kids put your name down and grade you and write comments about you – very informative! (You will note that there is no student equivalent for teachers.)

Your relationship with the students

The impression that you make at the start of September is crucial. Many people are told when they are training that they must 'act' as though they are confident with a class and that soon enough they will be. Obviously you know this, having qualified and taught a fair few lessons already, but it's still always difficult not to want to be **liked** – it's human nature to want to be popular, or at least not universally loathed, and that can make starting out difficult. Part of what makes this even harder is the old adage 'Don't smile until Christmas', a phrase that is frequently bandied about during training. This may work for you, but I actually disagree with it and can't believe that anyone would follow this 'advice' in a strict fashion.

There is a vast difference between being **liked** and being the students' **friend**. There is nothing wrong with the former – in fact, it can be very helpful – but it is befriending the students that may lead to disaster. I know of one teacher whose own arrogance led him to believe he could be 'mates' with the kids in his classes, and he used to contact them outside school. Clearly this is a big no-no. For starters it is inappropriate (and think back to the tale in the previous chapter about the flirting girls and accusations that can be made against you), but also it sets the wrong tone. You don't want to start a power struggle in your classroom, but nor are you having your friends round for a chat or trying to make the students like you.

There is always a very fine undercurrent in a lesson, one that is hard to sense even when you watch it being taught. Often, the lessons that look easy to us, for example when you're first training and you observe a teacher, are actually the lessons where the most management is going on. The class have the benefit of a great teacher with techniques that are barely detectable to the inexperienced observer. It is only when you are in the position of teaching that you can feel where to pull the strings and where to loosen others in a carefully orchestrated routine. This is probably why some people who are not teachers and have no experience of this career go wrong in assuming the job is a doddle.

Now, none of this of course is to say that you have to be liked – but in general, if you begin immediately to build a relationship with the students and to therefore gain their respect and trust from the outset, you are going to have a far easier time of it. The usual consequence of this is that you will be one of the popular teachers at school. Not in the sense that the kids want to be your mates, but in the sense that they know where their boundaries lie and that they can't push them – and at the same time, they will enjoy your lessons and be open to wanting to learn. The following are quotations straight from the mouths of kids who were asked to explain what made them behave in certain lessons rather than others, and what they liked or disliked about those particular teachers.

'She shouts all the time. I can't stand that squeaky thing she does with her voice – I don't listen, I switch off.'

'We get to have a laugh but none of us crosses the line. Probably because we know where the line is – he makes it clear – and we get down to work.'

'We spend about 90% of the lesson doing the talking and thinking. At first I didn't even realise how much we were learning in her lessons because it seemed like we did all the work – but I suppose that's the point, isn't it!'

'When I heard that Mr . . . was retiring I had to get in contact. It's twenty years since I left school but he made such an impact as a history teacher. He could be terrifying if you were out of order or crossed the line but commanded such respect. His teaching has had an impact on me for years.'

'She wears lovely floaty skirts and always listens to us.'

'He is just the coolest teacher – his sense of humour is wicked.'

'You can voice your opinions. She makes it seem like the lessons are *ours* and not hers. You can speak to her about stuff that isn't to do with lessons too. She doesn't take herself too seriously and she's open-minded. She seems to actually give a t*ss.'

'He goes on about himself all the time and what he did before teaching, like boasting about things he did in the army. Do I care?'

'He makes it more fun and I like having fun. He dresses up too. I like dressing up.'

'He doesn't shout very often – but when he does it's scary and you learn your lesson!'

'She only *threatens* a DT – who cares about threats? You can do what you like.'

'Mr . . . is great – just don't get on the wrong side of him! He always sends postcards home to congratulate us on good work.'

The one message that really stands out in all of these is that there are key elements that kids like and look for in teachers, and that those teachers who display these characteristics are the ones they will work for and work with:

- A sense of humour
- Treating students as human beings
- Not shouting
- A consistent approach to sanctions and rewards
- Building students' self-esteem
- Listening to students
- Allowing students the ownership of their lesson
- Setting out clear boundaries and expectations
- Having consistent and specific class management techniques
- Caring about students
- Wearing 'floaty skirts' (OK – not a requirement, but that comment makes me smile and just goes to show what close attention is being paid to you whilst you walk around your classroom!)

The funny thing about this is, that whilst we are engrossed in teaching we often don't realise what an impact we might be having on the students all around us. It's so easy to forget what it was like being at school ourselves and just how much you do go home and speak about the teachers to your parents, carers and friends. I loathed maths when I was at school. I was terrible at it and managed to get away with doing very little about it all the way up until I left. I don't think it's a coincidence that I also loathed every maths teacher I had in secondary school – not because they were terrible human beings, but because I knew that they were allowing me to slip through the net because this made their lives easier. And it's true – it is easier to ignore the kids who need more help. They are the ones who will take up more of your time in terms of differentiation and seeking out the SENCO and speaking to parents, but they are also the ones who will make your job **rewarding** – and you will be amazed to find that one day, when you move on to your next school, many of those kids and their parents will remember you, send cards and messages of thanks and tell you that you have been an inspiration to them, when all along you will have felt as though the kids wouldn't even remember you once they'd left your class. Things like this and moments like that make everything seem worthwhile – and, on a more selfish note, putting in this effort will make your life easier in terms of discipline and class management.

To complete this section on whether or not the kids will like or loathe you I am going to repeat a tale I was told during my PGCE year. This is something that happened to an experienced teacher with a 'challenging' class and I have remembered it ever since. It goes to show that we are all human beings and that relationships in classrooms can be built upon the most unlikely of foundations:

A friend of mine who had been teaching for years was an English teacher in a secondary school. She had a particularly difficult GCSE group and knew that she had to present a love poem to them. It was actually one of her personal favourites and she knew that she was going to have to get them really settled first. This could usually take quite a while so she was well prepared and waited and waited until the moment was perfect to begin reading it to them.

The class sat in total silence and she began. . .the poem was meant to start with the line 'And so, we kiss and part', but unfortunately the words that actually came out of her mouth were, 'And so, we piss and fart'. The class sat for about one second in total shocked silence until they started laughing – so hard that one boy fell physically out of his chair and on to the floor. They were weeping with laughter and my poor friend had to leave the room eventually whilst the students gained some control over themselves and she allowed her cheeks to return to a normal colour. It's the impromptu moments like that in teaching that can make your relationship with a class!

This tale goes to show that we are all human: at times, you will make great big fat blunders, but very often this can be a good thing, even though it won't always feel like it at the time.

> **tip** **Some secondary school teachers that were very honest admitted that they had taught classes for an entire year and had still not known *every* student's name with confidence.**

Your first lessons

These can be daunting, but they can also be very exciting. You need to make an impact and get things off to a flying start – and, hopefully, you want to stand out from the crowd and make a real impression on the students. A lot of that is going to come naturally to you because by now you'll have your own style. This is the time where you can stick with that for a while if you want to because you'll find that as the year progresses you will be evolving your teaching style without even realising it. On the other hand, you can stick your neck out and try out anything you like – you can experiment and give new things a go. With luck you'll have decent technology at your disposal, too, so if you didn't learn how to use things like VLEs and PowerPoint and so on when you were training, then now's your chance.

Whether you are following a strict SoW set out by your year group or your department, or have decided to follow the lesson objectives but are doing things your own way, you can use a variety of techniques and ideas to make your lessons exciting and motivating. The first lessons, of course, are usually disrupted by the giving out of exercise books and other small jobs that need doing. Class management may be playing on your mind. Either way, you can do things soon that are a bit out of the ordinary and introduce a sense of excitement about learning. It's all very well sticking to tried and tested methods for your first few lessons, but you can't do that for ever. This is it now: your chance to truly begin defining who you are with your very own classes. You won't be passing the buck any more, and even if you share classes you are still an individual teacher in your own right – so as soon as you feel able to, go for it!

The first thing you need to do is start learning a few names because you'll probably have seen your class list or lists well before you see the class, so we'll start there and then work our way through a few of the things you can do to get off to a great start with your students.

Learning names

This can be very easy for some teachers and not so easy for others. It can also depend on what school you work in and whether it's secondary or not – some secondary school teachers see **five hundred** kids a week – and there is a chance that you may not know each and every name with total confidence for quite some time. This can be very difficult when it comes to writing reports or even managing a class: we have very little chutzpah with a person whose name we do not know. However, there are techniques, and here are a few that you can try if you're finding those first few weeks difficult:

1 Snoop about and look at the names of the students on their **exercise books**.
2 Have the students fill in and stick in a little **'ID' sheet** at the front of their book complete with interests, hobbies and a photo of themselves.

3 In a tutor group, look at the names on **homework diaries** when you sign them.
4 Call students up to you one by one from the register for whatever reason and see them **face to face**.
5 Use name-learning **games**. Ask them to tell you the name of the person sitting next to them and one interesting thing about that person.
6 Get the students to tell you their names each time they answer a **question** – or get them to refer to someone else's point by name before voicing theirs.
7 Tell them you're rubbish at learning names because you're so **old and doddery** and get them to keep repeating them!
8 Find the school's '**mug shot**' book of student photos and photocopy your class/es.
9 If the school has an **online register** it's likely that the pupil's photo will pop up on screen as you tick them off.
10 Use a **seating plan** – make one with photos if you need to.
11 Does the school have an **online data delivery system** with all students listed? Very useful as it may have photos as well as SEN information.
12 Have the students make **name cards** that they take out of their books each lesson.
13 Give them **stickers** to wear, but make sure they don't wind you up with bogus identities.
14 If it's **parents' evening** and you don't have the foggiest who the person is that is standing with their mum and dad in front of you, then smile brightly and ask what time you had them down for, scrolling down your list looking puzzled but then alighting on their name as they say it. (At this point it also helps to have made detailed notes from each student's work and exercise book so that you can actually give an accurate report on their progress. It's one thing not knowing them by sight, but not knowing a thing about their work really would be inexcusable!)

In the end, there is nothing wrong with good old-fashioned **honesty** here. Tell the students (as in point 6) that you see hundreds of pupils a week and that you are new at this particular school and that you apologise for not knowing all of their names immediately but say that you'll do your best. If part of building a relationship with them is acknowledging the fact that we are all human, then they may as well recognise it from the outset.

Class and behaviour management

Generally, you are going to have had a lot of experience by now in dealing with class management. You will know that until you have class management sussed, you won't be able to do anything much with the students. This isn't to say that you should expect to be able to control every class you encounter because you won't necessarily be able to, and that doesn't mean you're a weak teacher. After all, students are human beings and they have bad days and some have home lives that are – quite literally in many cases – illegal. You can build relationships with those students, but that will take time – and sometimes it is never going to work. This doesn't have to be a reflection of any kind on you.

Some people seem to think that managing classes in secondary school is always harder than managing those in primary school. This is a sweeping judgment. It's certainly true that most teachers I've spoken to are daunted by the idea of whichever sector they are not involved with, but this all depends on the school itself and the classes you are given. In secondary school you do at least know that you are going to have a fifty-minute or an hour's lesson with a class and that you can then pass them on and breathe again if the going was tough. In primary school, you may have a class that are 'challenging' when at their best – and you will need to see them all day, every day. One teacher I spoke to recently made the move from primary to secondary after ten years:

It's not as bad as I thought it might be! Some of the behaviour is appalling but I see the kids for fifty minutes and then they go. That can be the longest fifty minutes of your life, though! In terms of work in school, secondary seems harder, but in terms of preparation and work outside school, it seems easier. (So far at least, but then I haven't had to do a continuous round of parents' evenings or reports yet.)

Obviously this is just one person's opinion, but it is interesting to speak to people who have experience of both. Many primary teachers get a great deal of satisfaction from their work that can be lacking for some secondary school teachers. A primary teacher can get to know their students incredibly well in a shorter space of time and may find more short-term rewards: looking back over an exercise book, for example, and seeing the vast improvement that they have directly contributed to in a child's work. Secondary teachers can take longer to see this kind of improvement or may even have to wait until exams are set. Either way, the first step towards any of this is class management – and it can feel wonderful when you finally start to get somewhere with a group.

tip **Don't feel disheartened after a bad day or lesson – see each new day or lesson as a brand new start. Modify your ideas as you go. Evaluate your teaching and try new techniques to see what works. Ask other teachers with the same classes what they they done – don't be afraid to ask for advice or admit to difficulties.**

There are certain key points to bear in mind when it comes to managing a class. Some of these result directly from your relationship with those students and are built on trust and consistency. Some of them therefore have been mentioned in the 'Relationships with Students' section as it is no coincidence that this is one of the standards that you'll have needed to tick off during your placements and will have to focus on again in your NQT year. The following is a list of ideas that will aid your class management:

1. Wait.
2. Be confident.
3. Set your expectations.
4. Have routines.
5. Be consistent.
6. Speak the whole 'language of choice' that you'll probably have come across in your training.
7. Use your voice and face carefully.
8. Use praise.
9. Work the room.
10. Explain.

Wait

First of all, you need a class to be quiet: this is the first step. Someone at university will have told you that if you wait for long enough, eventually all classes will settle and be quiet. **This is a lie**. I do not know why this lie is told. You can't make sweeping statements like that in teaching because it can be unpredictable. However, it is good advice as a first step. In actual fact, most new classes will eventually hush down out of sheer curiosity – they need to work you out and see how they can push you and what they can get away with. In fact, some classes may wait a few lessons before kicking off and really testing your boundaries. That's why you need to make them clear now, and the first boundary is **no speaking when you are**.

You should have some kind of phrase that you usually use to signal that you want quiet (see point ten as well here). An example is 'Stop talking, thank you.' This a firm command, but it is polite and automatically assumes that the students will do what you have said: you have already added the 'thank you' so, rather like an estate agent trying to close a sale, you're making it seem as if they are going to be in no doubt but to do as you say. Then you need to wait. And perhaps waaaaiiit and waaaiiit. Cue hideous moment to see if they become quiet. Usually a few will and some others will go like dominoes. Others may test you already – in which case, reiterate your point and do so whilst being confident.

Be confident

They don't know if you are nervous or not. They don't know whether you've been teaching for five minutes or fifteen years. Act as though you are fully in control.

Do not say anything else (e.g. instructions) until they are all completely silent.

A mentor of mine sat in my class once and held his pencil up at the moment when the students were all silent and I had waited long enough to be able to begin to gauge just what I was waiting for: you should be able to hear a pin drop.

To complete the domino effect, look at the clock. Look at your watch. Ensure you are standing firm at the front of the class. Write '1 minute' on the board (some students will realise this means they'll be staying back for that long afterwards) and increase it if needed. You can even get a big plastic stop-clock that the students can see clearly, stick it to your board and press it to time how much of your time they are wasting. Once they are quiet you can plan when you'll be getting them back at break so that you can waste **theirs**.

Do not utter a single thing – no introduction to yourself, zilch – until they are **silent**. If you begin and one of them talks again, stop immediately. Usually other members of the class will moan at the individual in question.

You may feel like a total prat when doing all this waiting – it can be a painful business. Perhaps you will encounter a class who will never be quiet even if you waited until hell froze over. If this happens even after several lessons, you can start calling in the big guns (HoD etc.) and seeking their advice – but this situation would be rare, so do not worry at the moment. Just wait it out! You are starting as you mean to go on. They will grow accustomed to the fact that you mean business and that this is the way things work in your lessons. If an individual refuses to be quiet, go and speak directly to them saying that you will need to send them out for two minutes if they cannot stop talking. Don't humiliate them whilst doing this; just be firm.

Set your expectations

Aside from the obvious need to set high expectations and for the students to aim high (think back to those standards again) it's also crucial to do this because these are **your** expectations of them; not every teacher will be the same. Some teachers just aren't good teachers and do lack discipline. The students need to know how you expect them to work and act and they need to know that you are in this with them – not against them.

Common courtesy is to be expected in your classroom. If a student were talking to you, you would not just ignore them and chat over their head to someone else, therefore you expect their full attention just as they expect yours. You need to introduce yourself to them. Have your name up on the board or around the room somewhere and go through a couple of classroom rules – not hundreds of them, of course, but the basics.

I have observed a lesson in the past that involved an AST (Advanced Skills Teacher) doing outreach with another teacher who had a class that were really worrying her. No matter what techniques she tried nothing was working, and so the AST was asked to help. The entire fifty-minute lesson was spent with the

AST speaking about expectations and the consequences of behaviour and responsibility and ended with her giving out a 'contract' to the students. The tone by this stage was one of real positivity and of teamwork, and the students decided on their **own classroom rules, expectations and consequences for their behaviour**. They then wrote them on their contract and signed and dated them. They were taking sole responsibility for this and worked hard to turn their behaviour around. This did mean that their usual teacher had to stick with it and remain consistent too afterwards, but it had a great effect on the students.

Some teachers feel that asking for help from another undermines them in front of the students. It depends how it is done and what you are comfortable with – but if we expect a team effort from the students, why not from ourselves? It is important for students to know that all the teachers in a school converse with each other and work together.

Have routines

Students need to know where they stand. Have the same routines. Wait outside the room for them to arrive, have a seating plan (don't give an inch on it unless there is a specific bullying or SEN issue and you know that it's valid), greet the students at the door, welcome them, have them sit down, ask for silence, take a register in silence and begin. At the end of the lesson have another routine: stand behind chairs, check uniforms, stop talking, face the front, wait for silence and then begin to lead out and so on. It doesn't matter what the routine is, but stick to it as the kids will come to know it and act by it. It also shows that you are in control and are calm and confident.

Be consistent

I stress this over and over again, I know, but it's so important! Treat all the kids fairly and use rewards and sanctions consistently.

Don't be tempted to start giving an inch here and there as you'll soon start to lose it – stick to the rules just as you expect the students to stick to them. Do not waver.

Speak the 'language of choice'

Always very useful: this helps you to give the students the **experience** of realising that their actions have direct consequences. In other words, aside from aiding your lesson control, this also teaches them one of the 'great lessons of life'. There are various ways of doing this. An example that you can say to students is along the lines of: 'I've given you a **choice**. Either you begin working as I have asked you to, or you will be in a lunchtime detention. The choice is yours.'

This is important because very often when you dish out a punishment to a student, they will whine that 'it's not fair, Sir/Miss!', or 'I didn't do anything!' This way, they have had it pointed out in no uncertain terms that the choice was theirs and therefore the fault that they lose their lunch/break and so on is also theirs – not yours, and it's not a case of being 'unfair'. In fact, it is the opposite: this is just. You are not 'picking on them' as a person or singling them out – they are being responsible for their behaviour.

On the other hand, you can show the student a direct choice. If you have Cause for Concern forms to fill out, for example, you can place one in front of the student on their desk with their name written on it and nothing else (yet). You can tell them that the choice is theirs: either they stop talking/concentrate, etc., or you will fill it in at the end of the lesson and they will have to pick up the tab for their behaviour. If they meet your expectations for the rest of the lesson, they can have the pleasure of tearing it up and placing it in the bin. (With a particularly disruptive pupil or one in a truly foul mood, show them the form but leave it on your desk, otherwise it may end up getting turned into an aeroplane anyway.

You will know the kids and you will be able to judge what will work with whom. Trial and error is a great thing.)

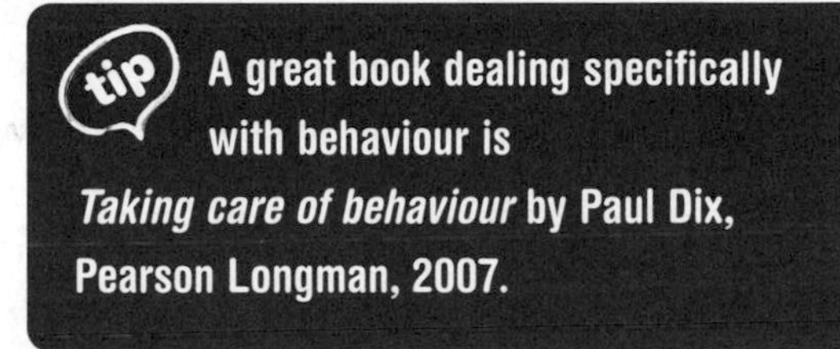

Another idea that is **fantastic** for placing the consequences of actions directly in front of students is one that a teacher I went to university with thought of. He didn't use it for very long, but I thought it was a great idea, adapted it, and went on to trial it with many classes and age groups. A primary school teacher has also used this with a class that he found very challenging at the start of the year and it worked extremely well, and the same happened for some NQTs that I have shared it with and also some cover supervisors, so adapt the following however you see fit:

STAR IDEA!

Escape Card/Golden Pass/Exit Card (any name you fancy!)

1 Make small credit-card-sized laminated cards. For some classes or primary you can personalise them for each child and put names or photos on them.
2 On one side you can put down a statement about classroom etiquette if you wish, e.g. 'The only classroom rule is that of courtesy to one another.'
3 When the students are lined up ready to come in to the class you hand one of these out to each of them, or you can do so after you have them settled and can then explain the concept.
4 **Explain it thoroughly (otherwise it can never work to begin with)**. The idea is that this card stays on the student's desk in front of them. It is NOT to be fiddled with and no other student is to touch another person's card or attempt to take it. To do so will have the consequence of — (whatever your usual sanction would be). If students behave and work as you expect them to (and be positive here, use phrases such as 'as well as you usually do', etc.), they can keep their card for the lesson. If,

however, anyone does not behave in an appropriate manner (again be positive about your expectations though), their card will be **removed**. They can **earn this back** through good behaviour, but at the end of the lesson (or day) students will have to line up at the door to leave the room and will not go until they have given you their card at the door. **Anyone who does not have it will stay behind**. If this is at break or lunch they can be held back for that time, or you will impose a different sanction on them.

5 Be careful to still be positive in your expectations of the students as you explain this. You can make a reward system up for those who keep their cards or (especially in primary) make certificates and so on to give out each Friday afternoon to those who kept theirs all week. Have a chart for names to go on. It can be used with tutor groups also – adapt it to your needs.

GOLDEN PASS CARD

Name ....

Class ....

Idea adapted from: Green, Gary: *Tips for NQTs – Behavioural Modelling* – the green card system. RE Secondary News, issue 37 (Summer term 2003).

In order for this to work you must be **consistent** in each lesson and consistent about when you take the cards and how to earn them back – and they can work **wonders**. For some reason the students love having a little credit-card-sized item that is laminated. It also means they see an immediate consequence of their behaviour. It means you can deal with minor disruption without disrupting the entire lesson in order to do so, and you don't need to remember the names of people who need to stay behind. I used this in an Ofsted-observed lesson when I was in the eighth week of my NQT year and the guy observing loved it: it even raises the profile of either you as a teacher or your department because the students talk about it and soon enough other teachers will hear about it. Give it a go – you can make great rewards systems with it and parents are usually impressed too. Most importantly, it can really benefit the learning going on in your class.

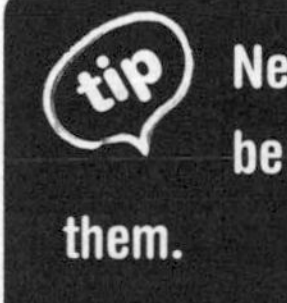

Never humiliate students. Do not be confrontational or try to belittle them.

Use your voice and face carefully

Don't be a 'shouty' teacher – you'll have little impact anyway and if you don't want the kids shouting then it's better to be quieter yourself. After you've screamed and hollered you've little else to do really and it gives the impression that you're losing control. However, do use your voice. Hopefully you'll have had some guidance on voice projection, and this can be very important for female teachers. As well as projecting your voice it can help if you learn to lower it somewhat. Very often you hear female teachers who become quite squeaky and high-pitched, which is never very useful! The way you use your face or even look at a student can work wonders without the need for even speaking, so do pay attention to what your face is doing. Don't be aggressive or confrontational. Don't give the students an argument to get into. There's a whole school of thought on separating the child from their behaviour as well: as a parent people often differentiate between disliking the behaviour whilst still liking the child. (In parental terms of course this means still loving the child but it's pretty unlikely you're going to adore your Year 6 students unconditionally to that extent!) Remain calm and in control. Once you've disciplined a student give them space to modify their behaviour, don't stay on their back. Keep an eye on them, though – if it starts again, begin to use further sanctions.

Use praise

This is obvious, so I won't patronise. Praise individual students, praise entire classes when necessary – build self-esteem from the outset. Use reward systems (see the Golden Pass ideas but also the following section on rewards) and make the pupils feel valued. Often the teachers who have the most success with students who are the bane of the staffroom, are the teachers who for the first time in a long while treated that student as a human being, recognising when they were making the effort, helping them to not be scared of making the effort in the first place. It's not naff or 'swotty' to try hard.

Work the room

You are there in a sense to entertain, so make the most of the space available to you. Use it and your body language to engross the students in the lesson and to motivate them. If a pupil is being disruptive, then even standing near them can put a stop to that. You can use the classroom as your stage. There will be times when you need to sit down and take a break, but these times shouldn't be in your first lessons. It's best to have a good handle on the students first before you do any teaching 'from your desk', and even then it should be done seldom in comparison to when you are on the prowl and moving around the room getting to know the students and engaging with them. By using the space available to you, you can make your classroom an entire theatre of learning. The following story is from a primary school teacher who was in Year 2 at the time:

> I transformed my entire classroom into a 'laboratory' for a science lesson and I dressed up in a white coat and big plastic goggles. I called myself 'Professor Honeydew' and taught the lesson by using different-coloured food dyes in water – the kids were sat on the carpet around me and loved it – they were totally captivated. Perhaps a little too captivated, because by the time I had removed my coat and goggles one little boy was in tears – he had wet himself and was sitting in the uncomfortable damp patch on the carpet. I asked him why he hadn't asked to be excused to go to the toilet and he replied, 'But you weren't here, Sir, it was Professor Honeydew'! Obviously my white coat and goggles were a more cunning disguise than I had realised!

Explain

Ensure that all of your expectations and any tasks and so on are fully explained. Ask if anyone has any questions. Explain again. Make sure that the students know what they need to do. This is just as true of any classroom 'rules' as it is of any tasks. Some teachers use a very effective '5,4,3,2,1' countdown to silence: the idea is that the students have stopped talking by the time you reach '1'. This becomes routine and the students know what is expected of them. An example of what can happen when you neglect to explain an idea such as this is the following story from a teacher that occurred when she first embarked on her PGCE:

STAR IDEA!

I had observed a lesson before ever teaching one where a guy used the countdown technique. It worked so well that I thought I'd give it a go – but because I hadn't been there when the teacher first ever used it, I didn't consider the importance of explaining what I wanted the students to actually do. Therefore, I shouted '5,4,3,2,1' randomly during their task and they just shouted back 'BLAST OFF!' and carried on chatting and laughing. A 'schoolgirl error' on my part.

So, simple as it may seem, do make sure that the kids know what you want them to do – and also let them know how long they have to do it in. Give them a time limit and return to that time limit, reminding them of how long is left before they need to finish. As usual, be consistent with it. Don't say that they have ten minutes and then forget it yourself and stop them half an hour later. Remember that with lower- or higher-ability students you may need different time limits just as you may need different tasks.

Rewards and sanctions

As was mentioned in the previous chapter you need to find out what the school policy is on rewards and sanctions and feel confident in what you are meant to use in any event. It's very important to know who you need to call and how to call them as well should you need SLT assistance and so on. This may not be confined to your lesson of course but also on duty or in the corridor. Don't let this worry you – it's pretty unlikely that anyone is going to misbehave so badly in your first lesson with them that you'll need to call on the help of the Senior Team – but you need to know what to do just in case, rather than stumble around and bluff things. (Although bluffing things is a skill that can come very easily to us teachers at times and is incredibly useful!)

In your first lessons it is very likely that the students will be testing you out just as they did when you were on placements. Make your expectations clear at all times and do not give an inch. Be calm and confident. The following are some ideas that you can use and also include the 'usual suspects' for sanctions. Do check those specific school ones though, especially in terms of paperwork you may need to fill out and pass on or file. In a secondary school in particular there will usually be a route that you have to follow in terms of sanctions, so I've applied a similar technique here. Your school one should be printed in your staff handbook and you may need to get an HoD or faculty to authorise after-school detentions and so on. A letter needs to go home to parents first in plenty of time as well so that they know their child is being kept after school. Usually there will be a rota printed of staff who will take the detentions after school.

Sanctions

Behaviour requiring sanction	Sanction to be enforced
Persistently late to lesson	Keep them back or have the student back at break for the time they missed.
Low-level lesson disruption (chatting, mucking about and so on)	Give a verbal warning with explanation of consequences. If it continues student can be kept back and spoken to.
Persistent low-level lesson disruption or Persistent not giving-in of homework	Cause for Concern filled out for file or given to tutor (always do the paperwork for file). Teacher to keep student in a short detention e.g. break time.
Escalating disruption of lesson, e.g. swearing (not at you), drawing other students in and against you, refusal to co-operate	Time out of lesson to cool down in corridor (the student, not you!). Cause for Concern. Department or year group detention with HoD or Head of Faculty after school. Internal department isolation. Phone call home. Put on report.

Higher-level disruption, e.g. swearing at you or getting up out of seat or being aggressive	SLT call out. Cause for Concern. SLT after school detention. Phone call home. Isolation. Day exclusion. Put on report.
Disruption in the corridor/at break/smoking on school premises, etc.	Very dependent on circumstances. Speak directly to the student if you can. If you don't know them or they run off, find out their name from someone else if you can. Call on other colleagues or duty team members. Pass the information on to the HoY or tutor. Cause for Concern.
Fighting	I've put this separately as it can be very hard to deal with and very intimidating. You can use reasonable minimum force depending on the level of fighting and can put out your arms and try to separate the students: easier said than done. Check with your own school for advice, and if you're pregnant or physically vulnerable in any way, stay well clear. If the violence is directed at you, remain calm and try to calm the student or just leave the area and find other staff. It's more important that you remain safe than worry at this moment about your behaviour-controlling techniques.

It is hard to write an extensive list of what can be termed 'bad behaviour' requiring sanctions because it would be filled with infinite possibilities, but this should give you an idea of how the sanctions escalate as the bad behaviour escalates. Remain fair and remain consistent. Often showing that you are 'disappointed' with a student's behaviour can work much better than showing that you are absolutely fuming. Remember how much worse it was when you were younger and your mum or dad said that you'd let yourself down and they weren't cross, just disappointed in you? This works just as well with kids who aren't your own.

Now, the nicer bit: rewards. The idea here of course is that we build a student's self-esteem, respect for their work and for that of other people, motivate them and encourage them and so on – all the stuff you'll have been told when training. The fun bit is in thinking of ways to do this. Your school may have specific rewards but that doesn't mean that you can't make up your own. Here are some ideas.

Rewards

STAR IDEA!

- Send **postcards home** for great work. You can order these now from some companies and the kids love them. Use the department or school budget and not your own, just find out how to do so first. Check with your HoD or other members of your year group. If you can't get postcards, type **letters**. Fill them in with the child's name and class or tutor group and hand them in to your reception or office. The staff there should be able to fill out the address and will then post them for you. They are a great surprise and I've had a number of parents contact schools saying how nice it is to receive good news like that.
- Use **stickers or stamps** whatever age the kids are – they love them. Hand them out in class, after class, on the way out of the door, whenever you like. There are some sticker companies that put codes on the back of the stickers so that the students can even register them online.
- Make a **sticker chart** for the students with their names on if you like or do individual ones for them. You could offer a **certificate** or something similar for each ten stickers that are received.

STAR IDEA!

- **Child of the Week**: a very good idea in primary schools. You can use this in combination with other things. A reward could be to take a **class mascot** home over the weekend. You could have a small notebook that goes home with it and the child can fill in their name, the date that they looked after it, and what they did.

- **Golden time**: used frequently in primary schools. Basically this is free choice activity time in reward for good behaviour.
- **Marbles in a jar**: my husband uses a technique in primary school with marbles in a glass jar that you can get the students to collect for good behaviour and to try and fill the jar. Marbles can be extracted for bad behaviour. You can then think of a specific reward for them. It encourages the class to work as a team.
- **Nominate students for prizes**. These can be given out in assemblies.
- Some students are shy about praise – give them a **personal reward** like a typed-up comment that can be passed to them discreetly.
- **Positive phone calls home**.
- **Positive emails** to their tutor, or Head of Year or Head of Department, who in turn can then praise the student.
- If an entire class have produced an excellent project or effort, get the **Head** to visit and congratulate them.

- Offer a **tutor or class trip** as a reward or incentive. Be sensible and realistic, and check with the Head or HoY first!

Basically you can just have fun thinking of rewards that you know the students will like and that you'll enjoy giving out. Be imaginative with what you do but, as always, be consistent.

Captivating lesson activity ideas

Use activities in your lessons that make you stand out from the rest. It seems a little patronising to sit here and write out a model lesson plan for you so I am not going to – you are a teacher and you've been doing that for quite a while now, so I think we all know what a plenary is and why setting out your aims is so important, but there are lots of activities that can be used to enhance learning, and it's always nice to hear about new ones. You may use some of these already but if not then give them a go. They become second nature, but funnily enough not all teachers bother. This only became apparent to me when I once went on maternity leave. A GCSE class made me a 'leavers' book' and all the students stuck in a photo and wrote something – and I was amazed that one of the things that had stood out to them was the variety of activities I used in lessons. I assumed all teachers did this, but maybe not. If you do already then that's great; if not, you might be interested in these ideas. A lot of that will depend solely on where you trained: during my training placements no one that I observed (and I now find this astonishing) ever used a single activity like these. I found out about them through friends and thought of others as I went along in my first job.

Community of Enquiry

I love this activity and there are a variety of ways to do it. It's fantastic for kids of all ages and it can be used during a lesson/to start a lesson/as a plenary – wherever it fits in your plan. The students should ideally sit in a circle, but use what room you have. You can give them a statement (it's a wonderful evaluation tool) and they have to say if they agree or disagree and why. You then need to press them further in their responses with high-order questioning, and their perceptive abilities are amazing once they really get going. You can also get them to respond to one another's arguments. This is good as well for name learning and it has similarities with circle time. It certainly begins to create a safe learning environment in which students feel comfortable and confident. It also provides the quieter pupils with a chance to talk. If someone wishes to pass you should let them – but usually, after a few goes at doing this, all pupils take part as their confidence grows.

Detective

In this activity you should generally have something for the students to find out. You can use it as a starter or anywhere else in your lesson, but you need to make some resources first in terms of clues that they can follow. They can work in pairs and you can provide them with a riddle or hide sheets around the room that they must find information from. There are plenty of internet sites that provide riddles that can be written up on the board to start a lesson or hide around the room. It's good for kinaesthetic learners too as they are up and moving around.

Image Enquiry

This can be done in different ways. You can have a picture on PowerPoint and slow reveal parts of it, or you can use an OHT. You can also have the kids in pairs and have one from each pair come up to the front of the room. You show them an image and they need to go back and start drawing it for their partner, who must guess what it is.

Kim's Game

This is the old game you used to play at parties when you were little. You place objects on a tray and cover it with a tea towel or similar. The students need to remember what was on the tray. This can be used to fit lots of different lesson aims as you may remove one item or have one added and so on depending on what you are teaching.

Vote with your Feet

This works best in response to a statement, e.g. 'Stealing is always wrong. Do you agree or disagree?' The students should move to one side of the room if they agree, the other if they disagree, and go to the middle if they are unsure. They should then be questioned by you to give their reasoning. As with the Community of Enquiry you can push them further and further and really open up the topic. You do need good management for this, although often the shock of being allowed to get up and move around keeps them quiet whilst listening to each other! It also shows that you trust them to behave and act maturely.

Teach One Thing

There is a statistic that says we remember a vast percentage of what we teach to someone else. Have the students stand up at the end of the lesson and tell the person next to them the one thing that stood out most to them from the lesson and explain what that was and why. Everyone should do this and if you have time you can push this further by getting pairs to join pairs and share learning, then feeding back to you. This can also be a starter to recap a previous lesson's learning.

Goldfish Bowl

This involves sitting some students in a circle where they have to face outwards and discuss an issue that you have given them. Another circle of students walks around them listening to their discussion and making points if they wish to.

Role Play

Some kids and teachers adore role play and it can be very good to end or begin a lesson and get the kids involved. They need to do so sensibly and with a very direct focus. Easy if you are used to teaching drama, but I know of some teachers who loathe this kind of technique and are not comfortable with it. Give it a go and see.

Hot Seat

This takes a brave student but can be a great activity. You can start or end a lesson with this or use it as a main activity. A student can come to the front of the room and literally take the Hot Seat. Other kids can question them about the learning or you can combine role play and have the student answer from a character's viewpoint and not their own. I know one teacher who has a specific seat for this activity and even plays certain music each time a student walks towards the seat. You can really personalise some of these.

Odd One Out

My best example of this is a history teacher who used to put a jelly baby, a poppy and another random object on her desk. The students had to guess the odd one out – which was actually the random object even though the students usually thought it was the jelly baby. Her topic was 'War' and jelly babies were originally known as 'peace babies' during the First World War. She also made sure that she gave some jelly babies out as rewards at the end of the lesson.

Chinese Whispers

Another children's party game, of course. It can be great fun as a starter, though do make it clear that no swearing etc. should be used and all comments should be appropriate!

Optical Illusions

You can find hundreds of these on the internet if you type 'optical illusions' into a search engine. They are great for starting a lesson and can either fit a specific aim, e.g. looking at viewpoints or perspectives, or can be used to get kids thinking. Also, you can find ones based on images that are central to your theme. The very fact that all the kids are looking at the same picture but are seeing different things – yet none of them is wrong – is a good way of students exploring the idea that you don't have to all agree on something, it's OK to disagree and it doesn't mean someone else is wrong just because they don't see (or think) the same as you.

Gimme 5

An easy starter or plenary: have the students give you five things that they have learned during the lesson or from the previous lesson.

Post-it Notes

A fantastic resource! You can write out answers on half of your Post-its and questions on the other. You can then stick them under the students' chairs. Halfway through the lesson ask them to look under there (amongst the chewing gum, no doubt) and get them to match up with the person who has their missing question or answer. They love the fact that these have been hidden there all along. (A word of warning is to ensure that they have stuck securely.)

Tips for thinking of your own ideas

- Convert **childhood games** (Kim's Game above is great, but different drama games or memory games can be really motivating).
- Have an object such as a **toy** in class to encourage listening skills. Students can only contribute to discussion and speak when it has been passed to them and they are holding it.
- Use things like **Post-it notes** in lessons to get the kids to write opinions on and **stick on the board** etc.
- **Use things that kids like!** A friend of mine starts a lesson on trust by leaving a plate of pre-counted sweets at the front of the

room and seeing how many are gone by the time she returns from being 'called away' by a colleague.

- Convert **adult games**. I am unsure how to phrase that without making it sound like a hideous innuendo, but things along the lines of writing the name of a character on a sticker and then sticking it on a child's forehead. Their partner has to get them to guess who they are by asking questions with yes/no answers.
- Use **card tricks** if you know any or **riddles**. I teach nothing about maths but my grandmother told me this when I was young and I was fascinated. I've used it just to get a class thinking:

STAR IDEA!

'Think of a number and don't tell me it. Double it. Add 10 (you can use any number here, different each time). **Divide by 2. Take away the first number you thought of. I bet your answer is 5.' The answer is always half of the number you asked them to add**. They love working this one out.

STAR IDEA!

- Get kids to **work in groups** with big sheets of sugar paper to share and formulate ideas.
- **Convert TV shows**. 'I'm a Student, Get Me Out Of Here', 'Dragons' Den', 'The Apprentice' – all have fantastic potential. You can make PowerPoint presentations that are like 'Blockbusters' or 'The Generation Game' to use for memory testing.
- **Interactive whiteboards**. If you have one (or even a projector) you can get music clips off the internet such as the countdown music from Channel Four's 'Countdown' game show.
- **Make up ideas to suit your individual lesson**. In a SoW about violence I've had the kids sat in a circle and link arms. Three students are specifically chosen by the teacher to come outside the room and are told that they must find a way into the circle when they go back in. They go in on their own and each gets one minute. Minor force can be used (you can see the Health and Safety issues here, but they are easily overcome by choosing the right class to do this with). What they don't know is that the other students have been told to only let in a person who says

'Please' and does nothing violent. It's surprising how few think to use manners first.

- Have the students **choose their own plenary** if you're confident enough to do so. Have a list of them on the wall. This is also great AfL (Assessment for Learning) as you're automatically enabling the students to relate learning to the lesson aims and they understand what the purpose of the plenary is.
- Link activities to **thinking skills**. Things like categorising, evaluating, ordering, analysing, criticising and so on. Matching cards are easy to make and so are writing frames. Even Vicky Pollard's 'Yeah but, no but' can be used to get students to see both sides of an argument and to remember to do so in their work.
- Keep an ear out for **songs** that you can use that are relevant to the kids' tastes.

- Use **websites** like www.youtube.com – search at home if your school has a filter. There are surprising resources on here, even for teaching stuff up to AS and A2 (Plato's Cave from the point of view of Spiderman, anyone?) www.thebricktestament.com is also **well** worth a look: I won't spoil it for you, log on and check it out. The NASA website has some mind-blowing images on it that really capture the students' attention.
- **Traffic lighting** is well used: cut out red, amber and green cards. Get the students to hold them up to signal what they do or don't understand or what they are unsure about.
- **Mini-whiteboards**. If your department doesn't have some, make your own with laminated card.
- **Digital cameras and video cameras**. Hopefully the school have some that you can use, or maybe even your year group or department. The students love stuff like this and are experts at putting movies together.
- Use **experiential learning** and things like **candles** and so on to set a mood. It sounds very tree-hugging but it usually works very well at creating a special atmosphere (minus pyromaniacs, of course).

- Get them **up to the board**. It may sound simple, but most students still love writing on the board!

Share your ideas with other people – ask around and find out what they do.

Some people find ideas like these really easy to come up with, but if you don't then just ask around. The internet is also a very useful starting point because as well as looking at specific teaching websites (there will be some of those listed at the back of the book) you can type things into search engines and just go from there. It's full of resources and ideas that not every teacher in the school will be using – and not every teacher will use it how you use it. Find video clips and relevant stories or funky ideas that other people have come up with and use this to inform your own lessons and to stand out from the crowd.

So – those are really the basics for your first few lessons. Before you know it, September will be over and you will be well on your way to settling into your new school. This is a really exciting time and gives you such a great opportunity to make an impact with your teaching and on your relationship with the kids. From here on in you can begin to build on these foundations and just get even better as the year continues. Teaching should always be a continual cycle of self-evaluation and progression: don't be afraid to try new things as you go on and to just learn from those that don't work. Only by doing this can you hope to become the best you can be, both for yourself and the students.

Chapter 5

Your first half-term

This section of the timeline is divided into two chapters, dealing with your first half-term and then the Christmas build-up. Chapter 5 will focus on the following:

- NQT induction
- Meetings and directed time
- Relationships with other members of staff
- Monitoring and assessment; and
- The half-term break

The following chapter will give further advice on:

- Planning and time management
- Relationships with students and parents
- Parents' evenings
- Keeping a check on your health and how to set cover work; and
- Festive ideas for the build-up to Christmas

So, if you find yourself needing advice on setting cover in the first half-term, or there is suddenly a parents' evening upon you, you can always flick ahead now to Chapter 6!

Doesn't time fly? Before you know it, you'll be into October. Your first September will be over and by the time that the end of your first half-term is approaching, you'll either still be running on adrenalin or you'll be begging for the break. Either way, by now you will be far more into the swing of things. Even if you don't *feel* as if you have been completely on track, you'll notice that you were once you go back to school after half-term and have to ease back into the rhythm again.

> **tip** It is extremely common for teachers – especially NQTs – to become ill with colds and viruses the very second that they stop and rest. Do bear this in mind if you are making plans for half-term.

At this stage, you should be more au fait with your timetable. By this I do not necessarily mean the academic timetable of lessons – for secondary teachers in particular this can take months to learn – but rather the school day. You'll know when your assemblies are held and where, you'll know when staff briefings happen and when you have to do break duty. It's a great feeling once you're more confident in your surroundings.

> **tip** If you're still getting lost around a secondary school then the best thing to do is ask a student: Year 7 are very useful for this as they too are still learning their way about.

NQT induction

To begin with then, we'll take a look at the NQT induction process. Presumably by now you realise that before you can even become an NQT and start your induction, you must have done the following:

1 **Obtained your QTS** (Qualified Teacher Status). This is part and parcel of your training and means that you have passed your GTP/PGCE/BA QTS and so on. You'll get a certificate at some point to say that you have QTS. **Keep it safe**: you may need it for any jobs that you apply for in future.

2 **Passed your skills tests**. I always found it slightly irritating that I needed to pass these tests despite already having GCSEs in Maths and English, not to mention a degree. The tests are in numeracy, literacy and ICT skills. Your university will have spoken about them and chances are that by the late spring, just before qualifying, you had already sat and passed them. If for any reason you are reading this before getting a job and before sitting the tests, a word of advice – go on the practice website first. The ICT test in particular has a different layout to the shortcuts that you may be used to using on a PC and it's worth having a go online first.

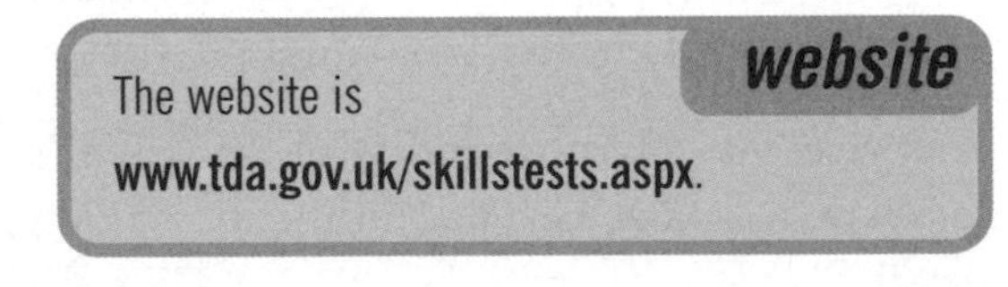

A general overview of the NQT induction year, before we go into more detail, is as follows:

Term 1

- Show your mentor/Head (almost always your mentor) your **Career Entry Profile**.
- **Formal Assessment 1**: have a formal observation that is the backbone to the formal assessment carried out by your mentor who will fill out the appropriate paperwork.
- **The Head reports back to the LEA or the ISCtip** (Independent Schools' Council Teacher Induction Panel) detailing that you are meeting the core professional standards. (You'll remember those from your training!)

Term 2

- **Formal Assessment 2**: have another formal observation by your mentor who will fill out the appropriate paperwork.
- **The Head reports back to the LEA or the ISCtip** detailing that you are meeting the core professional standards.

Term 3

- **Formal Assessment 3**: have yet another a formal observation (often done by the Head at this stage; see further on for more detail).
- **The Head will report to the LEA or the ISCtip** about whether or not you have met the standards and they in turn decide whether or not you have passed the induction period and write to the GTC (General Teaching Council) and the Head confirming their decision. You'll then get a letter from the GTC.

That gives you a basic overview of the year and what to expect, so let's have a look at each part of the induction process in more detail.

Passing NQT induction

As an NQT, one of the things that may play on your mind is the fact that you actually need to 'pass' this year: there are still a few hurdles for you to overcome before you can feel entirely confident and secure in your position. However, this is nowhere near as scary as it sounds. The following was said by a primary school teacher and sums up the thoughts of many teachers who have completed their NQT year:

When I first started training I didn't even know that there was such a thing as an 'NQT year', nor that it had to be 'passed'. At first this just seemed to add more pressure – I even assumed that the university still had a role in passing you. However, having looked into things further and spoken to tutors at university, I realised that it's more a formality. The people responsible for passing you are your mentor at school, the Head Teacher (who has very little to do with the process), and usually the LEA. All it really comes down to are three things – lesson observations, self-evaluation, and the same kind of standards that you had to meet in your training.

It is very rare for a teacher to fail their NQT year. When this has happened, generally the person in question would have been an extremely weak teacher to begin with, and one who had barely scraped through their training. The above example highlights the main issue here – lesson observations – and you have had **plenty** of those by now so there's no need to be fazed.

tip In some schools you will also be able to attend 'new staff' induction meetings. These cover all aspects of the school's policies: you may meet the SENCO, the CPLO and so on. Very useful indeed, so take the opportunity to go along to them.

The induction process

This will vary according to where you teach but will follow a similar structure. In order to find out fully about what the NQT induction process is for your area or school, the following will help:

website **www.tda.gov.uk** is very useful for this.

1 Research on the web: check out union websites (mentioned in Chapter 3) or look at the education sites listed at the back of this book.
2 Ask the school if they have a printed or electronic version of the induction programme.

3 You should be given a booklet advising you of what is expected and when: deadlines for observations and so on to be sent to the LEA, for example.
4 Speak with your mentor or induction tutor. They will be the person who will be organising you and working out when to do observations. If they are not doing so, then speak to the person 'above' them. **There is usually one member of staff who oversees all of the NQT inductions and ensures that paperwork is sent off on time**.
5 You should have induction meetings to attend with other NQTs and attending these will help you to sign off your standards.

Your induction mentor

This is the person who will help you through the year. They will do the paperwork with you when necessary and the observations. The paperwork usually needs to be sent off termly and you should be given a copy for your records. The school will also keep a copy. Your mentor is the person whom you can turn to for advice. Usually one would hope that a person who is a willing mentor is going to have patience and encouragement where needed – if this is not the case, then see point 4 above. At the end of the day, though, if all is not rosy in terms of your relationship with your mentor, follow the same guidelines that you used when you were training. Keep your head down, get on with the job, and get the NQT year passed.

The length of the process

This will take a year if you are full-time. If you are part-time, it will be worked out pro rata: in other words, it will extend into your second year until you have completed the same amount of service as a full-time employee. So, if you work a 0.5 timetable (half a timetable), it will take you two years to complete it. Bear in mind that you don't have to go into your NQT year as soon as you qualify: some people simply feel unable to once they have finally reached the end of their training. However, it is probably a better idea to get stuck straight in now than to leave it. At least that way you don't need to try and motivate yourself to get back into it and you're also up to date with what's currently going on in education.

Lesson observations

Generally there will be three formal lesson observations, and it makes sense that these take place towards the end of each term. The first observation, however, usually takes place within the first month of term. In most schools your mentor or tutor will do two of these observations and the **Head will do the other**. This may sound a tad frightening – up to this point it is unlikely that you'll have been observed by a head teacher before – but again, it's just another observation. You'll want to do your best as you should with all observations, so just go for it. Look at it as an opportunity to show off. Be sensible and do use activities that you're used to and that the kids are used to, but give it all you've got. There's no point being shy by this stage.

As well as these three formal observations you will most likely be observed several other times in your NQT year – once a half-term – and normally by your mentor. However, your line manager (who may or may not be your mentor) will also have to do a 'spot check' observation on you. This will happen **every year**. Sometimes you'll get a loose notice period, e.g. 'I'll be popping in some time next week', and other times you'll have no idea until they drop through the door.

In my NQT year I was signed off sick for two weeks after Christmas having run myself down beforehand and succumbed to a nasty dose of flu. I remember my line manager telling me to take it easy when I got back, so I spent the week setting independent learning tasks and getting back into the swing of school life. I was pretty shocked therefore to see her stroll through the door one morning after break! I was just setting up a video for Year 8 to watch and she announced that I was not to worry but that she needed to do my observation! I turned the video off and was amazed to find myself just winging it suddenly, making up aims and activities on the spot. Never before had I needed to do so but it was like water off a duck's back – I guess you don't realise how accomplished you are until you're in a situation where you've no plan to rely on. I managed to get a grading of 'Very Good' and was amazed – it did wonders for my confidence. – A secondary school teacher, now a head of department

---

Induction meetings

Your mentor won't attend these with you and they'll usually be held after school once a week. Sometimes different speakers from around the school will come in to see you to explain certain policies or ideas. An example would be a member of staff who is very experienced in organising visits and planning residential trips, or someone who is in charge of analysing data such as SATs results. This is a great way to learn about the school and helps to tick off standards. It also helps to see the other NQTs regularly as you can offer each other support. Do, however, watch what you say: you may wish to have a bit of a moan or a gossip, but as ever check who else is around. The following example is from a mature NQT who had been teaching for several months at the time of the incident:

In one of our last NQT meetings the Chair of Governors came along to ask us if there was anything that could be done for future NQTs in order to help them to settle in further. He's a lovely guy and I assumed we were all chatting informally and that I was still being professional. I suggested that perhaps NQTs could be trained in how to deal with incidents that happen in corridors and not just those in the classroom. I commented that it would be a help if the senior team were seen more often about the place and at this point a couple of other NQTs agreed. One said that in his last school the SLT had worked on a rota and patrolled the school. The Chair of Governors said that this was a good idea and I expected to hear no more – until the following week when the Head called me into her office. Our comments had been fed back to her and she had taken offence at my suggestion, even going so far as to say that I was attempting to make it a 'cause célèbre' amongst other NQTs. I was astounded that she should take it as a direct criticism of herself. I'll be very careful in future about who I talk to.

The point here is that in fact the NQT was making a very good suggestion indeed – and the Chair of Governors agreed. She did not then go and drop the NQT in it with the Head; instead she was putting forward what sounded like a reasonable idea. What would have been even better is if names had not been mentioned or if suggestions had been taken in confidence. As I've mentioned before, you need to be very careful about who you talk to and what you say.

Career Entry Profile

Here comes a bit of bad influence, but it is entirely honest: the teachers that I have spoken to have no clue where their CEP is. This includes those who have had meteoric rises in their careers and have had promotions coming out of their ears. In fact, I couldn't find even one teacher who still had theirs, myself included. Instead, when it comes to jobs and finding one, most of us have simply filled in the application form and sent it off. Some (myself included again) have kept a separate **portfolio** of evidence of our own, and this is always a very good idea. Tuck inside any details of courses you have been on, any training days and any examples of greatness on your part. This can eventually include

TAR
DEA!

examples of when parents have written into the school thanking you – because you'll be surprised at how often this can happen. There are many people out there who truly appreciate a good teacher and you may as well keep the evidence for others to see.

Generally speaking, your CEP is a document that is made much of when you are completing university – and during your NQT year you will have to fill bits in and set targets for yourself. After your NQT year you are supposed to keep it safe. I leave that up to you!

Leaving your first job whilst completing the NQT induction

This should make little difference to completing your NQT year, especially if you stay roughly within the same area or county; you just continue at your next school. You don't even have to complete the NQT year in one go. Do bear in mind that if you wish to teach at an independent school you will need to check with them and the LEA about completing your NQT year as they may need to liaise with each other, or the ISCtip (Independent Schools' Council Teacher Induction Panel).

An example of someone leaving their first job only a few months into their NQT year was mentioned in Chapter 1. The teacher in question simply went to her new school and they continued the process for her. After all, schools are full of people who have been mentoring NQTs for years, and most of them have it down to a very fine art. There will always be people who know what they are doing and you can ask questions to your heart's content – this is **your** NQT year, and if you are unsure of anything, don't be afraid to ask the people who are there to support you.

Self-evaluation

When I was training I would get bored witless with having to fill in a SEF (self-evaluation form) for each and every lesson that I taught. I would find myself repeating the same things on them over and over again. Whenever we had a day back in university the rooms would be full of trainees, all scribbling frantically to fill in a term's worth in one go, and make it look as though they had been writing them diligently for the past seven weeks or so.

However, as soon as I began my NQT year – and no longer had to take part in the over-the-top 'SEF for every lesson' torture – I immediately became aware of how valuable and crucial an exercise self-evaluation really is. The point is of course that you don't need to write a great list after every lesson of things that could be done better, because you've been doing this for some time now. Instead, you will have the clarity and confidence to know what is working, and what is not, **whilst you are doing it**. I always believe that the best teachers are the ones who make their lessons look easy. These are the teachers who are fine-tuning as they go along, picking up on the undercurrent of a class that a lay person who is merely observing cannot sense. In this way, teachers are 'conducting' a room full of students, and eventually we reach a stage where we can change what we have planned on the spur of the moment because we know instinctively what will work better. Long gone are the days when you needed a written lesson plan stuck in front of you on a desk somewhere, and long gone are the days when you needed to write out a SEF for each lesson that you've taught. Instead, you can now adjust your activities and aims as you go, depending on what has worked and what hasn't. You can experiment in the privacy of your own classroom without someone breathing down your neck the whole time, and you can continually improve your practice based on this.

This is not to say, of course, that you shouldn't be setting yourself targets. Part of the NQT year – **and every year thereafter** – is about setting yourself targets and **continually reflecting on your practice and modifying it**. This is the only way to keep improving. What you will find yourself doing then is engaging in real self-evaluation and developing into a reflective practitioner – and this is the way to be a great teacher. Many NQTs enter their first year thinking that they are great teachers, which may very well be the case, but however good you are when you start, you'll be amazed at how much better you become by the end of the year. This continuous cycle goes on (or certainly should do) for the entire length of a teacher's career. A teacher should never forget that the students are not the only people who learn inside a classroom, and we can hardly expect our students to keep improving themselves if we are not willing to do the same.

Your rights as an NQT

> **tip** **Check out the teachers' pay and conditions document on your union website address (in Chapter 3, or at the end of the book).**

As an NQT you should still be 'protected' in much the same way that you were as a student. For example, the majority of schools, when working out timetables, would not give a vast number of notoriously challenging classes to an NQT. This is not to say that you won't have challenging groups or pupils – you should do, otherwise you can't develop your skills – but some thought should be given to your current level of experience. Another example is that some schools do not give tutor groups to NQTs (although you may prefer to have one), or they will ensure that NQTs are only used for cover if the situation is desperate. Much of this will depend on the kind of school you are in and also how sensitive they are to the needs of NQTs, but there are some things that you should be able to take for granted when completing your induction year. You should have:

1. A mentor or tutor who supports you.
2. Formal discussions and assessments at the end of each term in line with the induction process.
3. A timetable that is reduced by ten per cent in order to give you time away from the classroom to further develop your skills.

(In all honesty this may eventually have to translate as 'marking or planning'!)

4 Ten per cent PPA time (Planning, Preparation and Assessment). **All** teachers are entitled to this. Under **no circumstances** should it be taken and used for cover or similar. Usually, especially if you work in a school where there are good proactive union reps, you will not lose this time: it is a statutory right. However, I have worked in a school where occasionally it would be taken. This is more often the case in primary schools, and I recently had a conversation with a primary teacher who is an NQT, during which she said the following:

I am currently owed around three days' worth of PPA time – that is how much has built up over the year. The school is small compared to a secondary and often we all just have to help out if someone is away. We don't have union reps here and in any case, I think it would be easier to speak out against the system if we were in a large secondary school. I'd feel too conspicuous and too much of a trouble maker if I did that here. We just get on with it.

This is all very well, but it is **your right** to that time. You aren't being a 'troublemaker' by being assertive. If you feel able, then always stand up for yourself. Do so professionally and in a polite manner, but be assertive and make it clear that you know where you stand. Your induction mentor should help you with situations like these if necessary, or indeed your union rep. Do bear in mind that even if there is no rep at your school, you can contact a local one via the website, who will help you if needed.

So that, in a nutshell, is a guide to the induction process for NQTs. At the end of the day there is a 99.99% chance that **you will pass** – so don't even bother stressing about it! It's just a way into the job that keeps you protected for a bit longer and ensures that you keep developing and evaluating your practice.

Whilst we are on the issue of what your 'rights' are within schools, it is also worth having a look at meetings and directed time. It is very true that you are expected to do certain things after school and you should prepare yourself for this. Often, during the first half-term, not much goes on. Everyone is having a bit of a settling-in period after the summer, students included, but this will step up a gear after the first few weeks and it is important that you know what is expected of you – and what isn't.

Meetings and directed time

Just as there are those people who believe INSET days provide us delicate teaching souls with a little constitutional holiday, there are also many who believe we finish work at 3pm. Hmm. I am pretty sure that you would beg to differ here. I am always fascinated by how people imagine teachers get any work done if they are strolling out of the door at 3pm, and doing nothing until 9am the next day. Although I suppose that's the point – they are assuming we **do no work**!

Far from popular opinion, then, the likelihood is that you are starting your day closer to 7–7.30am and that you are leaving school nearer to 5.30pm. Of course, when you get home you can probably hope to squeeze in at least another couple of hours to your day, if not more, making your grand total approximately twelve hours a day. That's sixty hours a week and it doesn't yet include weekends and 'holidays'. A damned sight more than the average forty hours a week. No wonder you may be feeling shattered by now!

A huge amount of this time is actually your own. We are not paid by the hour, and you won't get any overtime for the vast amount that you do, but some of the graft that you put in after work is actually time that your contract says you must – and it is known as 'directed time'. This may depend on your position in the school. A website

You can look up info on pay and wages (and much more) at: **www.teachernet.gov.uk**

person with a TLR (Teaching and Learning Responsibility point on their salary) is likely to attend more meetings, for example, than a classroom teacher. Usually schools try to separate the meetings when they are working out the calendar for the year. Normally this calendar is written and ready to publish by early July and often it is the Head's PA that is in charge of overseeing it. The best thing that you can do is make sure that you have all of the dates in your diary (as mentioned in Chapter 3) so that you know what you need to attend in advance. This is because although most schools are sensitive to the needs of their staff and schedule one meeting a week as they are supposed to, others will decide that as long as the year **averages** one meeting a week, they have done their duty. This can be very difficult to juggle at times because you may be the kind of teacher who prefers to do most of their work at home (for instance, you may need to collect your kids first and bath them and put them to bed before working again late in the evening), and you may have no access to childcare. Another problem may arise if your school holds twilight INSETs and you are expected to stay late several times per half-term. However, if this is an issue for you then at least you can bear it in mind the next time you look for a job (as is detailed in the jobs section at the start of this book) because it's often not something we consider when first applying.

The timing of meetings

A meeting should last for one hour. If a head teacher is present they will usually ensure that it lasts for only one hour so that they do not incur the wrath of the union rep. If a head teacher is not present, it may well go on for longer. This will sometimes drive you mad and at other times you'll know it's worth it and won't mind staying. I knew one teacher who was so in tune with his rights that he would leave a meeting after an hour even if it hadn't finished, and simply stand up and walk right out! I'm not sure I'd have the nerve to do that – even if I felt that I was sat there wasting time as can occasionally happen – but the following example is one that most teachers would sympathise with:

I had attended a year group meeting which had started at 3.15 pm and so I had expected it to finish at 4.15 pm. I live quite a distance from the school and knew that I had to collect my daughter from nursery by 5.30 pm. The clock kept ticking on and by 4.45 pm I was in a total state of panic as to what to do. Eventually, when the meeting still showed no sign of stopping, I interrupted, explained the situation and left. The Year Head was OK with that but apparently a few others stood up after I'd gone and also left, simply declaring that it had run way past their directed time. The Year Head was less than pleased with their attitude and I felt that I'd initiated a mass exodus!

Content of meetings

tip **Try to always attend meetings on time. Take a pen and paper with you and anything else that you've been told to bring. If it's a small meeting with people you work closely with, take some biscuits or chocolates or offer beforehand to do the tea and coffee.**

Sometimes you will attend a meeting that is very important or very useful indeed. Often these are the ones where you feel that progress is actually being made or that it is of some direct or practical use to you. You can expect to be given:

An agenda (before the meeting)

Any relevant photocopies (before or during)

A copy of the minutes (after the meeting – sometimes worth filing)

At other times, you will unfortunately have to attend a meeting just for the sake of it. You can usually guarantee that there will be at least one person there who will keep piping up with comments that have no real bearing on anything, other than to treat the rest of the staff to the sound of their own voice. Alas, this is the same as meetings everywhere, and it will be no different in school, but it is amazing how much time can be added to a meeting simply through inane waffle. Hopefully the person chairing the meeting is in full charge of it and will step in before it gets taken over completely. Try to make a point of only contributing valid and necessary opinions, as you will be noticed for this. Make yourself heard and be seen to have relevant contributions, but don't fall into the teachers' trap of talking too much – everyone wants to get home at some point!

Types of meeting

You will be required to attend various meetings and the following list provides some examples. Some of these are appropriate for all teachers; others are those you would need to be 'signed up to', such as a working party. However, do not sign up to too many! You will need all the time you can get at the moment for your actual teaching, marking and preparation. There is no point wasting time on attending voluntary meetings, especially in your first year, unless it is crucial to your career development at the moment.

Tutor group/Year group

Departmental/subject

Planning

Pre/post Ofsted

Full staff meeting

Faculty meeting

Gifted and Talented

Heads of departments

Pastoral heads

SEN

Staffroom Association

SLT

The list is endless, but this gives an idea of those that you will hear about as the term goes on. A full staff meeting is far more common in a primary school, and they are held regularly due to the smaller number of staff attending and contributing. In secondary school they are more likely to be held once a term, usually at the start of the academic year and the start of each term thereafter.

Open evenings and so on

The other area that counts as directed time of course is that of after-school events such as open evenings and parents' evenings. There will be more specific information about the latter further on in Chapter 6, but it is worth bearing in mind that these may begin at different times depending on where you teach. Many schools start an 'evening' at around 4 pm and will finish by 6.30 pm or 7 pm. Other schools cater more towards parents finishing work and will not even start until 7 pm. This can make for a **very** tiring day as they will continue until about 9 pm. This happens more in secondary schools than in primary. I imagine that this is due to the (old-fashioned?) thinking that mothers with kids at primary level don't work and so won't have to take any time off for a 3 pm appointment. Either way, evening events don't happen very often and the dates are always published well in advance. However, if you are expected to work until very late, do check on those pay and conditions again: there are guidelines about how much time you should spend in school before coming back again the next day for more!

It is also worth noting that of course if you teach secondary you are likely to do far more parents' evenings than if you teach primary. Primary teachers often have two a year, but these may each be spread out over two evenings to fit everyone in. Secondary teachers will have to do one or two for each year group that they teach.

By this stage of your first half-term it is unlikely that you will have encountered a parents' evening: even Year 7 tutors do not normally have a pastoral evening to 'meet the parents' until after the October half-term, and so there will be more detail about these and what they entail later on in this section in Chapter 6.

Relationships with other members of staff

After at least six weeks into the new term you are very likely to have begun forming solid opinions about the other members of staff. It is always interesting to hear the responses of new staff to other members, and the following are some comments made by NQTs from both primary and secondary schools:

I'm one of only three men teaching in a primary school and we all started this term. It's been really interesting to be in the minority for once. Several of the female staff seem to have just morphed into the 'alpha-male' role, often being quite domineering in comparison to the others. Myself and the other guys tend to keep a low profile at the moment – a true role reversal compared to the male-dominated office that I worked in before.

I work with a great range of personalities; some are very flamboyant and like to be heard in the staffroom and others are very quiet and say little during the staff briefings.

I love my new school – it's so supportive – the staffroom is more like a 'staff-womb'! I get completely mothered!

I guess it's like any workplace. Some people are exceptionally friendly and others are a bit reticent or even frosty. I don't know if this is because I'm a lowly NQT or if they're like that anyway – and I don't really care either because I just sit with my friends!

As with everything in school, it is better to suss people out before you begin making any of your opinions known (if your opinions are less than favourable, that is) because you don't know who is best mates with whom. It's best to go straight in with making a good impression, so here are some tips about building your relationship with the staff.

Be nice!

This may sound glaringly obvious but often – especially when nervous – we can come across as being very quiet, and this can in turn come across as being very snooty. You may seem frosty and uppity as opposed to shy and meek, and so it's best to allow your own personality to start shining through as soon as possible. This does not mean shouting out comments in the staffroom and throwing your weight around (some established teachers get very irritated by NQTs who seem a little 'ahead' of themselves), but just generally being noticed and being **nice**. Say 'thank you' to the people who have helped you to settle in. If the person in charge of reprographics has had to copy and laminate two hundred sheets for you, then pop a small card in their pigeonhole or email a thank you to them. Be especially courteous to the admin staff or your TA – they will be invaluable to you as the year goes on – and be professional at all times. Chat to the cleaners and make it clear that just because they're cleaning the room and not teaching in it, it doesn't mean that they are a less intrinsic part of the school than you are. After all, if you had to clean up all the mess from a school day as well as do your own job, you'd never leave before 10 pm. Smile and say 'hello' in the corridors, even if people don't respond (and this does happen, so shame on them!).

In general then, be friendly. Don't start being anybody's doormat; maintain your assertiveness, but be approachable and willing to learn. More experienced staff have a wealth of advice and experience to learn from and often pass on very good tips. It's too easy as an NQT to go in thinking that you're marvellous – and although you may be, you don't need to share that. I remember as an NQT having an Ofsted observation eight weeks into the year. I managed to pull off an 'outstanding' lesson and at the end of the week this was announced in the staffroom. Although I had been indescribably pleased – not to mention shocked – to receive such a grading, I was also mortified that it was read out. I made sure to lie low for a while afterwards for fear that other members of staff would assume that my head was implanted in my own bottom with smugness. At home I was elated; at work I was humble. It did wonders for my self-confidence in the classroom, though, because until then I had never assumed that I had the ability to teach like that, I'd just plodded along doing what seemed best to me.

Staffroom etiquette

You may have been warned about this before you even began teaching, so we won't spend too much time on it here – but heaven forbid you sit in someone else's seat in the staffroom! This is madness really: how else are you going to plant your posterior somewhere and how are you going to know who sits where? Just take it as it comes. Ask people around you if anyone is sitting there and just ensure that you never use a mug that isn't your own. Things like using milk need to be accounted for too: you may need to pay into a staff fund or you may need to bring in your own. The following anecdote is from an NQT who was a PGCE student when this incident occurred:

tip **Take an easily distinguishable mug into school with you to use. Make sure you have tea or coffee as well or find out about contributing to a staff fund for it.**

I remember clearly the time that all the trainees were called into a meeting with the professional tutor because it was felt that we should give up seats in the staffroom during the morning briefings. There weren't enough to go around for the permanent staff plus trainees as well, so we had to stand. We were then asked not to park in the car park due to a similar problem with parking spaces! I was really put out at the time but I suppose I can understand it more now that I'm a permanent fixture myself.

In some staffrooms, lots of people gather at lunch and break times. I always tended to be up in my room during the first half-term because I was too busy just getting back in the swing of things to stop for lunch, but by mid-November I'd be organised enough to go down and have some adult company. This was usually a real laugh and would set me up for the afternoon, so do try to get out of your classroom and speak to someone over the age group of those that you've been teaching for the day. This can of course depend on how long you get for lunch – it's often an hour in primary schools and about thirty-five minutes in secondary.

The state and decor of the staffroom can vary *hugely* depending on your school. Some come equipped with nice clean fridges and others look as if they are toxic waste dumping grounds. The following example is from a secondary school teacher who moved from an 'eleven to sixteen' school to an 'eleven to eighteen' school:

I had taught for several years in a school that really took care of the general environment, always painting over graffiti or muck in the corridors as soon as it appeared. They were just as fastidious with the staffroom – there was a pristine kitchen area with wooden work surfaces and appliances that the staff had raised the money for. Due to the fact that the environment around the place was nice, everyone – most kids included – treated it well. At my next school I nearly fell over during the interview when they showed me the staffroom. The general environment was pretty rough – nothing had been painted for *years* – but I'd expected more from a staffroom. The chairs were grim, there was a small 'kitchen' corner comprised of a cupboard that was falling off a wall and a rickety table, and the carpet looked like it had been laid in 1971 and used as a giant doormat ever since. Foul! I took the job but funnily enough I've never seen anyone eat their lunch in there!

This goes to show the vast difference between schools, so you may teach in a place where you would like to spend time in the staffroom, or you may teach somewhere where you would sooner hide with colleagues in a classroom and have your lunch in there. Either way, be as professional as ever. And do try to get some adult contact during the day.

It is worth noting here that most students would probably be gobsmacked by the way in which teachers talk in the staffroom. For starters, they seem to think that we don't actually discuss them amongst ourselves; but also, many teachers use atrocious language. This always made me laugh when I first began training and thought back to my own schooldays. I dread to think what names were used for my friends and me in the staffroom. The following is an example from a history teacher that relates to her PGCE training days:

I could never believe that teachers swore so much! I was in stitches about one of the older teachers who used to have nicknames for all the students, including one girl in Year 10 who was always smothered in both boys and make-up. He used to call her 'Mrs Slocombe' after the TV show *Are You Being Served?* and I could never look her in the eye after that.

The escape committee

This is the group of people in the staffroom who have become more than a touch bitter after years in the job. Unfortunately the stresses and strains of teaching can take their toll, and some people are just no longer motivated by it. This is not the same as having a moan after a bad day – these are the people who don't even seem to like the kids any more, and how can you teach if that's the case? It's best not to become too sucked into a conversation in these quarters because it depends on whether you want to stick up for your beliefs and opinions, or smile and nod politely and frequently as you try to appease the situation. On the other hand, you could point out in no uncertain terms that if it's that bad they should just leave – but that wouldn't necessarily endear you to anyone.

The dress code (is there one?)

There are stereotypes of how we expect certain teachers to dress and look. There are also some books about teaching that actually go into detail about each of these and simply reinforce the prejudice: namely, the prejudging of a teacher and their ability and style of teaching based on their style of dress. This really bothers me! In terms of dressing for school you need to be smart – of course you do. You do not, however, need to dress as if you were preparing to attend a funeral each day.

One of the most inspirational teachers I have ever met had the most amazing, one-of-a-kind dress sense. She was smart and professional yet still managed to look incredibly funky and quite cutting-edge in her style. I can think of several male teachers as well who take a real sense of pride in their appearance, with incredibly well-cut, contemporary suits and off-the–wall ties. I'm not suggesting that you go all out to do the same, but I am suggesting that you stick to who you are and what you want to wear. Just keep it smart.

For some male teachers there is an issue over whether they go for the whole suit, including jacket, or whether they stick to shirt and tie.

I very rarely go in wearing an entire suit, but I always make sure that I have a shirt and tie and that I model a smart dress code for the students – how else can we expect to nag them about their uniform? I also teach PE and dance and so some days I wear tracksuit bottoms and a T-shirt. If I had an open evening or similar on one of those days, though, I'd make sure that I took a change of clothes too. – A primary teacher

---

It is worth ensuring that you're comfortable in what you put on. I know some female teachers who always wear make-up to school simply because they feel more secure in themselves that way. Having spoken to a teacher training mentor recently I'd probably also recommend that one of the main things you can do is either try to dress in natural fabrics, keep windows open or smother yourself in antiperspirant. This is a mortifying tale and could happen to the best of us:

I had a trainee that I was mentoring a few years ago and she was very nervous indeed about teaching a particular Year 10 class. They were rowdy and she had issues at the time over class management, so we'd worked through various strategies beforehand. When it came to teaching them she was actually doing OK – but unfortunately her nerves got the better of her and she developed vast patches of sweat underneath each armpit. She had a close-fitting top on and as the lesson continued the marks became more and more apparent. Even after she had left the school for her next placement the students still remembered her as 'the sweaty one', bless her. Not to mention the fact that the following week she managed to get chewing gum stuck on her bottom and I had to point it out to her – but not before most of the beady-eyed students had already spotted it as well.

SLT – Last and by no means least

Your relationship with senior leaders should be a good working relationship. At the end of the day, you'll see very few of them on a close personal basis if you're in a secondary school, and you'll see a lot more of them if you're in a primary school. As usual, be polite and professional. You don't need to be told how to speak to members of the SLT, but the following tale is one of great comfort if you're feeling a little intimidated by them.

Our SLT team are fantastic. Very down to earth and grounded. I always remember the guy who became Assistant Head telling me that he hated it when some people spoke differently to him after his promotion. He said, 'It's just me – only I'm doing a different job. But it's still just me!' I thought that was a really inspirational comment.

So, although you don't want to be walking down the corridor and offering the Head a high-five, you can still chat when needed and you can still use your sense of humour appropriately. No one wants to be surrounded by a load of sycophants, but nor is there any harm in treating members of the Senior Leadership Team as if they were still human beings.

Monitoring and assessment

In amongst everything else you will have to do during your first half-term, you will at some point have to start not only marking the work of students but also monitoring their progress and assessing their work in order to inform further planning and differentiation. This is no mean feat and you need to stay on top of things. Remember that parents will see work and exercise books and will want to know that you are looking at them regularly. The following is a list of helpful tips and advice.

Tips for how to stay on top of your M&A

Find out about the policy first

Check out the school or department's assessment policy first to check you are on track. Check the calendar to see when actual assessments are due in.

Record progress

You can do this electronically or you can do it by hand. Your school may have a specific system that they like you to use or you can make up your own. SIMS is a system that is often used in schools and has an 'Assessment Manager' that you may be required to fill in termly with a level for work or progress.

Keep an M&A file

This can be just a folder or glorified 'mark book'. Print or write your class lists in it and every time you see a piece of work make a small note about the students' progress. This is a huge help when it comes to writing reports: you'll have something solid in front of you. You can then modify your teaching according to progress or lack of progress.

Collect books in

Aim to have a look through them once a fortnight depending on how many kids you teach. Keep it manageable, though. You can even look through them whilst they are doing a task by walking around the room.

Your questioning technique

There will be more on this in the Assessment for Learning info that will follow these tips, but you do need to develop your questioning technique. Have a look at the examples that are given because this is not only a way to teach your students but gives you fantastic insight into their ability and achievement.

Use your TA

If you are a primary teacher with a teaching assistant assigned to your class, do make the most of their skills and time. They can look through tasks that do not need assessing and sign the work to show it has been looked at.

Stamps

Have a stamp made with specific comments on it: the office can help you find out how to order one. Stamp class work to save time. You can even have a stamp made that has specific skills on it such as 'Analyse' or 'Punctuation' to tick off according to whether or not the student has demonstrated these skills.

Stickers

Use as many as possible! (See the rewards idea as well in Chapter 4.)

Use names

If writing a comment always refer to the student by name: personalise it. If they love Man United then comment (politely) on this. Show an interest in them.

Positive, improve, positive (PIP)

Begin your comment on a positive note, then include an area for improvement, then end on a positive again. Use this to target set.

Personal assessment policy

As well as the policy that is followed by the school, you can also print out a small list for each student to stick in their book about how you will mark. This can point out that all work will be looked at, some will be marked, some will be read, some will be assessed fully and so on. This means that parents will also see this and understand that even if each and every piece of work is not covered in your pen, it is still being read.

Assessments

These of course need more thorough marking and not just a tick. Be thorough. If a student has gone to the effort to complete the work, go to the effort to mark it properly. They do appreciate it.

Coloured pens

Use a pen to mark but don't necessarily make it red. Some people think that seeing their work covered in red pen is disheartening to students!

Codes

Use a code for marking with initials, e.g.: a 'D' in a circle could mean 'more detail needed'. Draw smiley faces and so on – just make sure the students know what code you are using. You could print it out and stick it in their books so that they can refer to it.

Spelling

Unless you are an English teacher or a primary teacher, do not correct each spelling mistake. If it's a technical term, correct it, if it's misspelt once, correct it. After that there is no need to keep doing so throughout a piece of work.

Oral assessment or presentations

You don't have to see a written piece of work in order to know how a student is progressing. Some students may work very well orally but have poor literacy skills. Always use your eyes and ears throughout your lessons to help you to monitor and assess as you go along. Set presentation work to help students with the spoken word and to help you to assess them without a mound of paperwork in front of you.

Marking online

Lots of VLEs (Virtual Learning Environments) give you the ability to mark online. You may prefer this or you may loathe it. Stick to what you like. Some teachers prefer to have the work printed and in front of them; others are not so good at collecting paperwork and prefer to have things emailed. You can set a task on a VLE and mark it online without ever having a hard copy if you wish. Your school or department should train you in using this software.

Assessment sheet

Make a sheet that is like a multiple choice sheet but detailing each part of the assessment with printed comments about what a student must do to reach each requirement. You can then just tick each box for the statement that most refers to the standard of work that the student has produced. This is similar to giving level descriptors in student-speak, but you can make it look friendly by using clip-art or images on the sheets.

Assessment for Learning: peer marking

(More on this in a moment.) Get the kids to mark each other's work. Give them a mark scheme and ask them to mark it and then write one comment about what is good and one comment on how to improve next time.

Tracking documents

Keep class lists and mark out the students' September levels and then complete termly – you can track their progression.

Model answers

Write an answer to questions yourself and demonstrate what is actually needed from the student in order to achieve each level or grade. You can even get them to mark these answers and say how they would improve them.

Levels

Obviously these need to be done, but they can be very disheartening for a student who is struggling so do be careful. Often a student looks at the level and not the comment. You can try and combat this by giving back the comments first and the levels afterwards to each individual with an oral explanation and words of encouragement.

The Benefits of Monitoring and Assessment

At first the task of monitoring and assessing can seem very daunting: how will you cope with so much to do? But the previous ideas should give you time-saving tips and strategies, and soon enough you will be in the swing of things. It's important to remember that you do not have to mark each and every written piece of work in detail. In fact, some of it you will just skim through. Save the real marking for assessments, and when you mark these give it your all. It's really crucial that you make students feel their work is valuable to you. This can do wonders for your relationship with classes.

I was astounded a couple of years back when a GCSE class received some work back from me and then said that whereas I had clearly gone to the effort to mark their work and comment on it, their history teacher had only ever marked their coursework. Not a single practice question or any other piece of work had been looked at – ever. How can you teach like that?

The chances are that this lack of professionalism would be picked up on by a school. Many departments, year groups or faculties either moderate work or spot-check exercise books. If you were to be visited by Ofsted, your books would certainly be checked. You cannot teach properly if you have no clue as to what your students are producing, but do not panic about this straight away. In time you'll get to know your classes very well even if it doesn't seem like it right now. This is only your first half-term – by Christmas you will know them much better, and after that there will be no stopping you. One benefit that primary teachers have is their close contact with students: you will know those kids inside out by the time next July is here.

tip You may hear people speak about two types of assessment, 'summative' and 'formative'.
Summative = Occurs at the end of a unit and is a final assessment of the students' work.
Formative = Ongoing – you assess the work during a unit and give specific areas for improvement and advice, highlighting weakness and strength, setting targets based on this.

Assessment for Learning

The vast majority of schools should by now have AfL policies or may be taking part in whole-school initiatives for AfL. If you have not heard of Assessment for Learning, then in very basic terms this means that the students are actually learning from the assessment of their work and that it becomes something **meaningful**. Depending on your age, you may be able to think back to your own schooldays and realise that you were never once told what the actual aims of your lessons were – did you know exactly what you were doing and why you were doing it? When assessments were given back to you, did you know what your grade really meant and why you had that precise grade and not another? And did you know what you could have done specifically to improve upon it? The chances are that you didn't.

AfL is about more than writing a meaningless level on a child's piece of work: it's about placing an emphasis on the fact that the lessons you teach are essentially the **students'** lessons, and that they need to know what they are doing, why they are doing it and how they are doing it. They need to be able to evaluate their own work, and by doing so they can take independent steps to improve. This makes so much sense that it makes you wonder how it hasn't always been around – and in many ways, as with much in teaching, it probably has, but under different guises and never so apparent as now.

Examples of using AfL are about to follow, and you may or may not be surprised at just how many of these things you do already. You may not have realised that these are examples of AfL because a lot of your prior knowledge will depend on what you have learnt whilst training, and also where you trained. In fact, if you refer back to Chapter 4 and the lesson ideas there, many of those are good examples of AfL, which probably accounts for why they work so well.

Share the aims of your lesson

It just makes sense that if the students know what they are meant to be learning and how they are going to learn it, they'll be in a better position to judge whether or not they have done so by the end of the lesson/unit.

Return to the aims at the end of the lesson

Get the kids to tell you whether or not they have done what you proposed and how this has helped them. Get them to evaluate the lesson based on the aims – don't be scared of doing so.

Use writing frames

There will be an example of one of these in a moment, but by using written structures for arguments and so on you are helping the students to see what is expected of them and whether or not they are achieving it – and subsequently how they might improve.

Use thinking skills

Stretch the students. Activities that involve implementing thinking skills are those that get the students to:

Enquire

Research

Explore

Investigate

Create

Invent

Process information

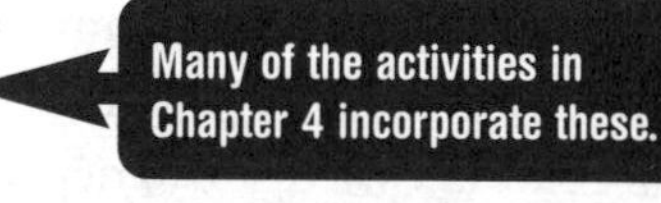

Explain

Reason

Categorise

Recount and recall

Reflect

Evaluate

Get the kids involved

This may also sound obvious, but activities such as Community of Enquiry (as mentioned in Chapter 4) mean that not only do the students listen to each other, but they actually **evaluate** each other's opinions, thereby stretching each other and showing each other how they could improve an argument. You can get the students to say how another person's answer can be built upon. This is useful for everyone and demonstrates why the creation of a safe and secure learning environment is also crucial.

Use higher-order questioning

Your questioning technique as a teacher is crucial. It's no good to just ask a question and be given a straight answer all the time. You need to make things more open-ended and you need to enable the students to be brave enough to go that bit further with their opinions. Often, if you ask a question and then just stand back, nodding thoughtfully as the student begins to answer but then remaining quiet, the student will automatically go on to fill the silence with further thoughts and opinions – which can be **excellent**. When they've done that, you then ask them **why**? Go further and further until they can think no more, and then get others in the class to build on what's been said. Move on to asking 'how?', 'but what if . . .?', 'demonstrate it for me' and so on. This can have fantastic results in both primary and secondary students. It is also especially impressive in a lesson observation.

Not enough teachers use higher-order questioning, so set yourself a target to be one of the those who do. Something called Bloom's Taxonomy is a list that was categorised and created by Dr Benjamim S. Bloom after he had researched hundreds of questions that are asked by teachers. This showed eventually that most questions asked by teachers relate only to **knowledge** and **comprehension** – but that the teachers who get the most from their students will go on to get pupils to **apply, analyse, synthesise and evaluate material**. These are the skills involved in higher-order thinking.

You can stick meta-cognitive questions such as **why**, **how**, **where**, **what if**, **when** etc. all around your room to keep them at the forefront of the students' minds when they are working.

Share mark schemes and set targets

If a student doesn't know the criteria for marking something or assessing it, how can they know which level to aim for, let alone how to achieve it? Give the students mark schemes that are in pupil-speak. They can tick these off as they work through an assessment after setting themselves a realistic target with your help. You can then refer to the mark scheme when you assess it.

> **tip** **One of the best things that you can do in your NQT year (and future years if you get the opportunity) is to spend time observing a variety of other teachers. Always ask in advance as some people don't like being watched, but it is an invaluable experience.**

Peer assessment (and also self-assessment)

Get the students to mark each other's work using a mark scheme in pupil-speak. They should go through the work in detail, just as you would, making comments about where they have reached targets, what has been done well, and how to improve. This benefits them in many ways: not only do they mentally compare their own work to someone else's, but they become more au fait with the way that work is assessed and this will inform their future work. Once the marking is complete you need a thorough debriefing with the class about what was done well, what could be better and so on. Refer specifically to the work in hand as you do so.

Level descriptors in pupil-speak

You can stick these up around the room. They need to be in language that the students understand and you can then refer to them when you need to. Allow the students to become accustomed to what is expected of them. Some teachers believe that levels can be very disheartening, so you need to go with the flow of your school really. If it's a policy that each child needs to know what level they are working at you are going to have to tell them – but you can do so in a positive light and you can use AfL to build their confidence and self-esteem, so resulting in an improvement next time.

Structured worksheets

If you are looking at, for example, a poem, you can type the poem in the middle of a worksheet and then place questions such as 'Why?', 'How does this make you feel?', 'What if this were you?' around it. Help the students to see how to respond and how to question something for themselves.

Model questions

Always model examples of answers for the students. Write them yourself so that students have a direct example and comparison between levels in front of them.

Make a whole-class question

You can set a question and divide the class into groups. You can then get each member of the group to answer a specific part of the question – they can do this on different-coloured paper – and then stick their sheets together in order to make up an entire answer to the question. These can all be read out to the rest of the class once the groups are done and can be commented on as a whole class. You can then take the best separate answers and piece those together to create the best answer that you can – a whole-class effort. Ensure that you get the kids to say why they believe some answers are better than others.

As with all activities, this list could be endless: you can always think of more ideas and methods and there are likely to be many going on in your school at the moment. Things such as higher-order questioning are always used with gifted and talented students, but they should be employed teaching methods with **all** students. At the end of the day, a lot of AfL comes down to self-evaluation in the classroom. It enables students to take more responsibility for their learning and it enables teachers to facilitate this. In many cases, it also makes for more exciting lessons too. I once heard of a guy who had an 'Assessment for Learning corner' in his classroom: I never actually got to see this or had it explained to me, but I'll leave that to your imagination: It may be something you'd like to try yourself.

So, before we leave monitoring and assessment behind (and move on to the more relaxing issue of what to do for your half-term break) here are three practical examples of the above ideas. They can be very easily modified to fit the year group or topic that you are teaching.

A writing frame for an evaluative argument

I use this from Year 7 to GCSE, and it can be adapted to whatever you like. The students usually have a mark scheme with it and mark each other's to begin with. Eventually they don't have a writing frame and it becomes second nature. It incorporates a mnemonic called WAWOS that some exam boards use (The Welsh Board, for example), and that I've also incorporated in a textbook myself (*Think RE! 1*, Brewer, Green, Lush, Mantin, Phillips and Smith, Heinemann 2005).

Students write one paragraph or so for each part of the framework and respond to a statement. They know that they need to write a well-structured, balanced, evaluative argument.

Statement: 'Religion is hypocritical. It preaches equality yet practises prejudice towards homosexuals and women.' Do you agree or disagree? Give reasons for your answer.

For a very low-ability class the statement and framework would be worded differently and there would be an additional column to the right so that the students could fill it in on the sheet, not on a separate page.

What?	***You don't need to write anything for this part: just think about what the statement is actually asking of you.***
Agree or disagree?	Do you agree or disagree with the statement? Begin your argument here.
Why?	Give as many **reasons** as possible for **your opinion**: at least three.
On the other hand...	Now consider why another person may disagree with you – **balance your argument** – think of at least three different responses to the statement.
So?	So? What is your overall **conclusion**? Make it concise.

Table adapted from Lovelace, Ann and Joy White. *Beliefs, Values and Traditions*. Heinemann, 2002.

Higher-order questioning

Using the same example of the statement that was used above, a question in class asked by the teacher could go as follows:

Teacher: Yes, Hannah, do you agree or disagree?

Hannah: I agree, Miss.

Without higher-order questioning you could just leave it here, thereby achieving very little.

Teacher: Why do you agree, Hannah?

Hannah: Cos you hear about it all the time, Miss.

Teacher: OK, but what do you hear about? Give us a specific example.

The teacher could ask the rest of the class here how Hannah could build upon her answer.

Hannah: Well, at the moment there's been loads of stuff in the news about the Roman Catholic Church and the issue of gay adoption.

Teacher: Right, good example and great to hear that you're aware of current affairs, well done – but how does that link to prejudice? What have you actually heard?

Hannah: That the Roman Catholic Church would rather close down adoption agencies than let gay couples adopt kids. That's wrong.

Teacher: Why do you think that it's wrong?

Hannah: Well, just because you're gay it doesn't mean that you can't raise children.

Teacher: How does that specifically relate to the concept of prejudice then, Hannah? What do you think the Church are doing?

Hannah: They're prejudging gay people, Miss, based on what their sexual preference is.

Other students put their hands up.

Teacher: Go on, Tom, how can you add to the argument?

Tom: But they might not be prejudging them on their parenting skills as a couple, they might just be going by what the Bible says is right and wrong.

Teacher: In what sense is that not a reflection on a gay couple's parenting skills, Tom?

Tom: Well, the Bible doesn't **specifically** state in a commandment that gay people can't be parents, but it does say that men shouldn't have sexual relationships with men – and gives examples of families that have a mum and a dad and kids. Maybe the Church are just following that.

Another student joins in.

Katie – But that is discrimination!

Teacher: 'Give me an example as to why or how it's discriminating, Katie.

Katie: Just because you don't agree with what someone does in the bedroom it doesn't make them less valuable or equal than you as a human being, Miss – and 'cos of that it doesn't make you a worse parent! Lots of straight couples are terrible parents.

Teacher: What if the couple were lesbians and not gay men? Would that make a difference at all? Does a woman's maternal instinct make a difference?

Tom: Now you're discriminating, Miss!

Teacher: No, Tom, I'm just having fun playing devil's advocate!

And so on.

In actual fact what the teacher is doing, of course, is facilitating an excellent discussion that could last for quite some time. The teacher is pushing and challenging the students further and further and they in turn are learning from one another. She could just have left it at the first hurdle – thanking Hannah for saying that she agreed and then moving on – but this would have achieved nothing.

The next thing to do in this case is to ask the kids what they have **not** considered from the statement. Some of the students will realise that the statement said, very broadly, '**religions**' – not just the Roman Catholic Church that Hannah picked up on – and also the concept of **equality**. The teacher should now lead the discussion onwards to tackle the crux of the matter.

Make a whole-class question

Again using the same statement as an example, you could now divide the class into groups of four. You could give each student in the group a different-coloured piece of paper – one for each part of WAWOS, for example. They can then answer their part, share it with the group, and then stick the pieces of paper in order, end to end. This creates one long answer.

You the teacher can then ask the groups to share their responses. The groups can discuss who has best answered certain parts of the question and why: for example, someone may have used a biblical quotation referring to homosexuality or marriage and children to back up their point. You can then put together the best bits as a class and arrive at the 'perfect' model answer.

This should provide you with some more practical ideas that you can modify yourself and put to use in your classroom.

The half-term break

Before you know it, you'll be there. It will be the last Friday of your first half-term, and by the time you come back it will almost be November. You may be shattered and just about getting up in the morning, or you may be on an adrenalin ride until the last bell goes. Either way, **you deserve a rest**! You also deserve:

Congratulations!

So, decide in advance what you're going to do in terms of work – preferably not too much – and try to get any work you are going to do out of the way as quickly as possible. You really will need a rest and a break, and unfortunately this may be your quietest half-term of the year when it comes to marking and planning. There is always work to be done during the holidays, but at least you can do it at home! If, however, you need to pop in to school, check the opening times beforehand. Most likely they are 9am – 3pm, but do find out before you travel in.

Many teachers – especially NQTs – do find that they become ill over the holidays. It seems to be your body's way of reacting to the sudden cessation of 'school mode'. The second that you stop your body just gives in, so take it easy if this happens to you. Either way you can rejoice in having completed your first few weeks – and you can start to recharge for the next seven or so. Onwards to Christmas!

Chapter 6
Onwards to Christmas

By now you are well into the swing of things. You have one-sixth of the year under your belt, you're getting to know the students, and you have the Christmas break to look forward to.

It is also around now that other issues raise their heads – parents' evenings, for example – and you will also need to ensure that you are working on your planning and time management in order to accommodate these further drains on your work/life balance.

In this chapter, then, you will find advice on the following:

- Planning and time management
- Mock exams
- Relationships with the students
- Parents and parents' evenings
- Keeping a check on your health and how to set cover work
- Festive ideas for the build-up to Christmas

Not long to go until your first two-week break! You'll notice that your relationship with the students keeps changing the longer you are at the school, so in this chapter we will examine this in more detail, and suggest ideas on how to cope with certain issues that may arise. An example would be the students who may actually seem to loathe you (though hopefully you are lucky and there are none of those) and the students who seem to like you a tad too much. It is also around now that you may have to take some time off, perhaps because of an NQT course, graduation ceremony or illness, so we'll take a look at the issues surrounding absence and cover work too.

tip Only seven weeks to go until the Christmas holiday. Pace yourself and try not to get run down. You can ease off a little towards the last few days of term – the kids won't want to work too hard and neither will you.

tip Decide whether you want to stay on at school and complete work or whether you want to take it home – you may end up doing both, but depending on how far you travel or family commitments, one or the other may suit you best.

Planning and time management

Where does the time go? You may well find yourself in a position now where you feel far more confident about juggling the expectations of the job, and in doing so you may also find that you seem to lose whole chunks of time. The weeks pass by in a blur, and before you know it there will only be a couple left before Christmas. This can be a great bonus to teaching: the half-terms are hard work and can be a real slog, but because of that hard work, they **fly** by.

You are in a position where, if you chose to, you could work every single hour of every single day and **still** have things to do. Clearly this would kill you, and you would be on your knees begging for mercy way before Christmas. However, for some of us the temptation is just too much and we work on and on, never giving ourselves respite and flagging towards the end of term. I am one of those people: my HoD in my first school was forever writing the same thing on my Performance Management Review targets: 'Must learn to take it easy!' Therefore, if you are one of these people (and even if you're not), some handy tips are needed.

The great art of pragmatism

So, how do you manage to balance your time? Chances are that the answer to this is that 'you just do'. Some teachers stick to a sort of timetable: they reserve particular evenings each week for marking and others for planning. Some teachers fly by the seat of their pants and hope for the best. It's no good therefore for someone to tell you how to work because we all do what comes naturally, but one sound piece of advice is to be sensible. **Be pragmatic**. Set realistic and sensible targets.

Set targets and prioritise

Question: If you have a pile of assessments to mark, a pile of exercise books to mark, and five lessons to plan, what do you do first? Answer: Choose between the assessments and the lessons as priority. When do the assessments need to be marked by, versus how many of the lesson plans are crucial and when do you need to teach them? If it helps you then make a list and work out what needs to be done and when it needs to be done by. Exercise books can wait a bit longer. The kids will be gagging to see their assessments, not their class work.

It may seem obvious to some people to work in this way, but sometimes you just can't see the wood for the trees.

Plan some 'desk lessons'

You don't have to make every lesson an all-singing and all-dancing entertainment session. Plan some lessons that involve text book work. This may not set the world alight but it keeps the students occupied whilst you sit at your desk and do more pressing things. If you have a class who are climbing the walls then clearly this isn't a wise option, but you can still dig out a DVD to show and link it in some way to your long-term objectives. Don't feel guilty about this. It's not the best example of teaching, but then you won't be doing it all the time – and if it's a choice between you taking it easy for a lesson/day, most schools would prefer you do so rather than risk your health and take a week off because you're so exhausted.

You can also set various forms of group work or project work that will keep the students on an independent task. This is no bad thing: some schools need to work at encouraging independent learning because students can become too reliant on being spoon-fed the information that they need. Just repeat this to yourself if you start feeling guilty, and take reassurance from the following tale:

On a PGCE placement the department that I worked in was the laughing stock of the school. The HoD had somehow managed to get away with 'teaching' her entire subject by showing video after video. The walls were lined with videos, the drawers were full of videos, and even the kids entered each lesson asking which one they would be watching!

You could never be this bad!

Assessment for Learning

Do bear in mind that one part of AfL is peer or self-marking. You can ask the students to look through and evaluate each other's work. As long as you have a full debriefing afterwards then not only is this good practice but it saves you some energy and some time. Have a look at Chapter 5 for detailed advice about AfL and its purpose and benefits in the classroom.

After-school activities

You need to be sensible here, particularly if you are a primary school teacher or a PE teacher, because you can end up staying late every night if you are not careful. You may wish to sign up for every extra-curricular club going, or to attend every working party that exists, but this will just drain your time. Choose carefully, especially in your NQT year. It can be so tempting to think that this is the way to kick-start your career and get noticed around the place, but your main focus for the moment should be to get the basics right. Join clubs, set one up if you wish, but don't join everything. You need to ensure that you can stay on top of your marking and planning and that you **still have a life after school**!

A word here about school performances. If you are a primary teacher or a drama teacher, the chances are that around now you will have one to prepare for. In both cases, some after-school work may be necessary, but much of your preparation can also take part during lessons. Do not feel as if you have to do too much: do what you are comfortable with. The established teachers at the school should be taking the brunt of the workload here – you'll get your turn for exhaustion in the years to come.

Paperwork

You will be given umpteen sheets to read and several hundred more to fill in over the course of the year. The vast majority can be chucked – you will not need them – and some need to be kept. Whatever you need to fill in, do it as soon as possible and hand it **straight back**. Get it over and done with. If it helps you, keep an in-tray on your desk for the bits you need to read, but the chances are that you'll still never look at them and will be shocked to see them still there when you clear out your rubbish at the end of the year.

Emails

You may well be working in a school that attempts to be 'paper-free'. If so, then you already know that what this actually translates as is **slight reduction in paper found in pigeonhole, vast increase in inane emails found lurking in school account**.

If your school relies on email, this can be good and bad. Pros include the speed of email, cons include the fact that you'll forget whatever you've read, such as information about certain students, because it's no longer there in front of you once you close your laptop. It's best to whizz through the emails and delete as you go. Print any that are worthwhile and reply as soon as possible to those that warrant a reply. Otherwise, you may as well cancel your teaching for the day because you'll spend most of it with your head locked in your laptop.

My school relies heavily on email. The fact that you can contact people at a moment's notice is great, but I get up to fifty emails a day. Around 5% of these are useful; the rest are along the lines of 'Has anyone seen my black gloves in room 32?' Very frustrating!

I like the ease of email, but it does make me lazy – I no longer have to chase anyone or move around the school, for example, to place a note in someone's pigeonhole. In fact, I can get away with spending entire days in my room with no adult contact at all. Is that a good or a bad thing? It's no wonder that I'm still clueless as to who half the staff are, I only know them as a virtual name on a screen!

I love email – I'm a SENCO but I'm completely chaotic where paperwork is concerned. The more electronic the communication, the better it is for me.

Plan a week in advance

I know I've said it before, but any further than a week in advance can be a waste of your time, and any less can be too little. Just keep on top of it. You'll have found your rhythm by now, or at least what works best for you. If not, then really do sit down with your planner and get things in order: life will be much easier.

Sunday evenings

If all else fails, do what your students will be doing – leave it all until Sunday!

Mock exams

For those secondary teachers among us, this is also the time of year when at some point the mock GCSEs will be upon you. This may be your first real experience of mass marking, so we'll take a look at the balancing act that is required at around this time.

There are a couple of guidelines that will make this easier for you. Rest assured that at least the mocks only come once a year and that you will see for the first time just how your students are going to perform in exam conditions. Some of the poor things will crumble under the stress, in which case you can take necessary measures prior to the summer; while others will forget to bring a pen and struggle to remember their own name. It is best to have this direct experience of the 'exam attitude spectrum' long before next May!

What's in the paper?

Ask your HoD what is going to be in the paper long before the kids will sit it. The chances are that it's a past paper that will be used. You could ask to see it at least three weeks in advance.

Plan your lessons

Once you've seen the paper, **plan**. Because the students can't do well if they haven't been taught the content, plan your next few lessons around what will come up in the paper. This isn't cheating: it's sensible preparation, and it will give them a confidence boost.

Practise exam technique and timing

This is a great opportunity because if you begin it now, by May it will be second nature. Make sure the students know how long they will have and practise some timed questions. Use past papers – ask your HoD for some.

Pop into the exam hall

Nip in during the exam. The kids loathe it if you snoop over their shoulders, but I usually do it anyway. If you do, make sure it's only over the shoulder of a student who is confident and make sure you don't linger very long. Students normally like to know that you care and that you've taken the time to pop down whilst they sit the exam. In fact, this being an internal exam, you may well have to invigilate. (You should no longer have to do so for external exams because the school should pay for supervisors.) Exam invigilation is one of the most boring activities known to human beings. Keep your fingers crossed that you won't get caught out too often.

tip **When invigilating internal exams (e.g. mocks etc. and not 'the real thing') you are allowed to take marking in with you or something to do. This is worth bearing in mind so that your brain doesn't freeze over whilst you are in there.**

My HoD and I had to invigilate an exam and after only fifteen minutes of stalking the aisles I was ready to pull out my own nails as a preferable form of entertainment.

I turned to look at him standing at the back of the room, and had to hold myself together when I saw him pull his tie up in a strangling motion, indicating that he too would prefer methods of torture to the silent exam hall horror. It was good to know that you can have a sense of humour in situations like that and not be regarded as unprofessional.

I remember invigilating a Year 7 summer exam and, to my revulsion, having one boy tell me that he felt sick. He usually lied as easily as he breathed so I hoped he was mucking about, but as I led him out of the hall he opened his mouth and threw up all over my shoes. I was traumatised!

Collect the scripts

These should be given to you immediately after the exam so that you can begin marking. The best thing to do if you've not marked one before is to ask your HoD for a **mark scheme**. This may seem to slow you down once you first get going, but you'll soon find a pace.

Mark them as soon as possible

Plan to mark them as soon as you can. Get it out of the way. It's definitely best to get them marked **before the Christmas holiday**, assuming that your school sit them prior to the holiday. The students will want them back and you'll want a break over the Christmas period. At this time of year and at the end of term, it's unlikely that you'll have any other urgent marking to do; though if it looks as though you will, plan to get that out of the way before the mocks are due. You'll want to give them your full attention. Don't go bonkers with comments as it will take you too long, but try to write a positive comment and a target on each.

Keep a record (there's no passing the buck!)

Record the grades in whichever way you usually keep your M&A. (There is more on this in Chapter 5.) The great thing about mocks is that you can also set individual **targets** and it helps you to know your students. It gives you comments for parents' evenings (see a little further on in this chapter) and also reports. These are going to be your first ever Year 11 cohort to sit an external exam in the summer and you are responsible for their grades, therefore use the information that the mock performances give you to your best advantage. Plan lessons around them, or revision, and pinpoint areas for improvement.

Work out your pass rate (ask your HoD for grade boundaries)

You can go so far as to work out averages and pass rates for your classes if you wish. Don't get depressed if they aren't what you wanted: the kids rarely revise at all for their mocks and things are usually much better in the summer. Your HoD may wish to know exactly how they've done or s/he may leave it up to you. You may also have an HoD who wants to moderate some of your marking. This can serve to reassure you that you're bang on track, or it can be a useful tool to modify your marking. Don't be scared about it – just take it as it comes and look upon it as advice for the future.

Set targets

Set your targets with the students in question, ask them to set their own and discuss these. Use the mocks to help you to get the best out of the students – and for them to improve and get the best out of their external exams in the summer.

Marking the students' work and taking the care to do so actually helps to build your relationships with them – the kids will appreciate the time you have taken. As your first term is nearly over your relationships will have changed since September, and so we will have a look at ways in which you can continue to build on them.

Relationships with the students

The relationship that you have with your students will keep on changing throughout the year. It began, of course, in September, but as time goes on subtle changes will take place. Some of these changes will not be so subtle, and many of them will link to how you have taught and managed the students since you first met them.

The first few lessons with any class are generally the ones where the students are sussing you out. You may find that they are quiet the first few times that you teach them – hence the importance of laying down your consistent ground rules from the start – and nearer to half-term (or sooner if you teach primary) they will have begun to test you a little more. The chances are that if you have been too lenient with a class, this 'testing' will have started quite early on, but there are ways to rectify the situation and we will have a look at these in a moment. All the relationships that you are building with the students will influence what your relationship with their parents will be like, and later in this chapter we will move on to consider parents' evenings and how to deal with them.

Too lenient?

If you feel that you've just been too lenient with a group – and you will know if you have – then you need to get the ball back in your court. The key to your management is that you cannot let any misdemeanour go, no matter how insignificant it may seem. The students will start to look for ways in which to test you out, and if you have 'failed' those tests they'll only push you further next time.

We all know that students need boundaries, it's just a matter of being brave enough and consistent enough to set them and keep to them. If your class or classes are taking advantage, you need to take things back to the beginning. Look back at the September section and the ideas for class management and then **start again**. It is never too late – go back to a clean slate. If you allow things to slide out of your control, not only will you make your life much harder, but you'll be doing the students a disservice too.

With classes who are low ability, keep trying new things every week until you find what works for them. I know one teacher who has an extremely low-ability Year 8 group and they have now fallen into a pattern for each lesson: they come in, have a brief starter followed by a brief discussion, and then a very structured worksheet. While they do the work they listen to music of the teacher's choice on his laptop. At the end of the lesson, they have a five-minute plenary. Now, this idea wouldn't work with every class – many would be bored stiff of following the same routine each week – but this teacher has simply experimented over and over until he hit upon what worked for them. It isn't necessarily the best idea for teaching and learning, but it is **best for this class**, and at least they **are** learning – something that they may not be doing otherwise. In some of their lessons around the school the children in question were running amok, so this story is a complete success in comparison.

So, with the class that needs to be reined in, do exactly that, **rein them back in**. There should never be a power struggle in your classroom: **you are in charge**. It can be very damaging to your confidence to feel as if you have lost a class before the year has really begun, but feign confidence and control and get them back where you want them. (The Golden pass/Exit pass idea in Chapter 4 could be put to good use here.)

Too strict?

Do remember that when you have the class controlled and you have been teaching them for a few weeks, you can then allow them to see that you are a human being. As I have mentioned, I am never a fan of the 'Don't smile until after Christmas' rule. If you are out in the corridor and you see some of the kids you teach, smile and greet them. Why not? This is the way to better relationships. Because of a lack of confidence we can sometimes come across as a bunch of humourless old grumps, and occasionally teachers start shouting too much simply because they feel tense about being 'the new one'. If you are too 'shouty', it will get you nowhere. Relax and be yourself. Keep the pupils within the boundaries that you have in place in your classroom, but don't make it too much of a military operation. Stay calm and approachable as well as clearly being in control.

You can't please all of the pupils all of the time

Sometimes you will teach a class that you have a great relationship with, but there will still be one or two students who seem to despise you. Due to the fact that the rest of the class are doing well, you will know that you have no need to worry here. As long as you can be certain that you are not failing the student in any way, then rest assured that it's not you – it's just the nature of human relationships. Sometimes you'll have this great relationship with a class that are actually the bane of another teacher's life – and the student who loathes you is only acting in this way because s/he can't believe that their mates are working and enjoying your lesson. They may be disappointed that there is no mischief afoot!

A problem for some secondary teachers can be jealousy in the classroom. Female teachers may experience 'Bitchy Adolescent Girl Syndrome', and male teachers may experience the 'You're an Attractive Male, the Girls All Fancy You, I'll Tell Them All You're Gay' response. You may well be gay – but this isn't going to stop the young ladies at school from writing your name all over their exercise books, which generally means that the spotty male youths in your classes are going to be rather put out. Students of all ages and sexual orientations fancy teachers of all ages and sexual orientations. As long as this occurs, some pupils (usually the ones who are used to being adored by their peers themselves) are not going to like you. You can't do much about it, but usually they'll come round as soon as they see that you have no intention of gloating and signing autographs in the canteen at lunchtime. Which leads us to the flirting pupils ...

The students who like you a little too much

Flirting students can be a real problem. Although the majority of this behaviour is harmless, it does need to be nipped in the bud. We all hear about stories in the press of teachers who have been entirely innocent yet had their lives ripped apart by false allegations before their innocence has been proved. On the other hand, we also hear about teachers who have been justifiably placed on a Sex Offenders' Register. If you suspect any colleague of the latter tread carefully: speak to your mentor or line manager first. If you suspect a student of lusting after you, follow these guidelines to keep yourself safe:

1. Never be alone with the student in question.
2. Always have the door of your classroom open.
3. Ask your mentor or a colleague to be with you and speak to the student about their behaviour. Your colleague can appear to be 'busy' elsewhere in the room so as not to humiliate the student, but you need a witness present.
4. Pass the issue straight to your line manager, school nurse, pastoral care team etc. and ask them to deal with it.
5. Never touch a student. This is easier said than done if you have a child who is distraught about something, but a student with a crush can read a lot into a meaningless gesture or comment.

6 Be careful about electronic communication: emails can be misconstrued very easily and it's best to have work emailed to your school account.

There will also be students who seem to develop quite an emotional attachment to you. These kids can seem like little stalkers – you'll turn around in your classroom at lunchtime and there they will be, waiting to chat and find out how your day has been. It's crucial to recognise that something may be going on behind the scenes that is causing them to try and form an almost 'parental' relationship with you – check with the school nurse or SENCO. These are also the students who may make a disclosure to you, in which case you must seek the guidance in Chapter 3 about the CPLO and how to deal with this. It could just be that the student likes you – in which case, be flattered, but move them on. Point out that you have work to do and that they have an entire playground to roam, not to mention the library if it's raining. Do be nice to them, though. Whilst you are not there to be a surrogate parent to your students, it's always funny in a sweet way when they accidentally call you 'Mum' or 'Dad'. (Especially if they are in Year 11.)

The safest rule of thumb in teaching is to remain professional at all times. I have stayed in touch with two of the students that I have taught since my career began – in just the same way that I have stayed in touch with my own secondary school RS teacher, because she was the person who inspired me to teach. I occasionally receive emails from the ex-students in question and it's always great to hear about how they are both doing. One is a girl that is now commencing her gap year before training to teach RS, and one is a boy who had a very tough time actually making it through school due to his own behaviour. I worked hard with his mum and dad to keep him in and he has now completed his GCSEs. It would be wonderful to hear from him in twenty years' time and know that he has made a success of his life. However, these are appropriate and professional examples. I have also known of a teacher who pushes boundaries too far and chats happily on MSN to his current students about what he is up to at the weekend. This is unnecessary and unprofessional. Keep everything fully above board – as I said in Chapter 3, there is a difference between being liked and respected versus trying to be friends with the students. The latter is never going to be OK.

Parents and parents' evenings

It can be fascinating whilst teaching to meet the parents behind the students in your class. Sometimes you can take an accurate guess at what those parents might be like and what their personal philosophy towards education and teaching might be. At other times, you'll be knocked sideways by the differences between the students and their mum, dad or carer. We'll move on to have a look at the issue of parents' evenings, but before doing so it's a good idea to consider your relationship with the parents via the students that you teach. The kids will be going home and telling their parents about you, so the first impression that a parent has comes directly from the child. This may be more reassuring if you have a half decent relationship with that child than if you harbour a secret loathing of them.

There is a huge difference between parental involvement in education at primary level and parental involvement at secondary level. If you teach in a primary school, the chances are that you'll have met many – if not all – of the mums and dads already. Parents generally wait at the school gate or on the playground and you may have to take your students out to meet them. You may well have faced a few issues already and not all of these will have been easy to deal with. The parents of students at primary level can often seem quite 'interfering' compared to what you experience when they are older. This is understandable – the child may be young and vulnerable – but it requires great patience on your part. However, seeing as you teach the same class of under-elevens every day for the academic year, most secondary teachers will be in awe of your patience already. The following tale is from a young male primary teacher:

Towards the end of each academic year, we meet the students from our class for the following September. There is an open evening as well during which the parents of the students can come in to meet us. I was really quite shocked last year when a mother came to see me and said that she didn't want her daughter to have a male teacher for Year 1. There were no background or SEN issues here – she simply said that I wouldn't be 'maternal enough'! I was very insulted and pointed out that it wasn't my place to be parental anyway – I'm here to teach. The mother wrote to the Head and was told that nothing would be changed, I would be teaching her daughter. It's a year on now and not only have I had an apology but the mother has thanked me for the education that her daughter has received over the past nine months. Most parents are pleased to see a male role model in a primary school but I guess you just never know!

At the same time, of course, you will get letters and thanks from parents who are truly delighted with how you have helped or inspired their child. This is always rewarding and makes up for the difficult parents that you may face. Many of the teachers that I have spoken to have received letters of thanks from parents that have been copied to the Head as well, and this display of thoughtfulness can make your day.

Occasionally you will come across the kind of parent that teachers dread. The next example is from a highly experienced female teacher who has taught in a secondary school for seventeen years. It just goes to show that however long you've been doing the job, you still face the same issues.

I taught a Year 9 class and told one boy that I'd move him if he misbehaved again. He started eating his worksheet so I took him aside and explained that I'd like to see him at the end of the lesson. I don't allow low-level disruption to pass because it leads to worse behaviour, so he knew that he would have to take responsibility for what he'd been doing.

At the end of the class I kept him back and told him that the worksheet was school property and that the school had paid for it – however small a cost that might be. I suggested that he either write out a new copy of the sheet or pay to photocopy another one. He agreed to this and left.

Five minutes later he returned – with his mother. Parents aren't allowed to just walk on to the site because of Health and Safety but luckily my HoD and another colleague were present to act as witnesses. The boy's mother was furious and spoke about how petty I was. She said that her son was a 'good boy' and that if a photocopy was 'only ten pence' then she'd give him the money to 'shut me up'. With that she flounced out and my colleague commented that we were merely trying to instil respect in the students. The woman turned around and shouted that we were a bunch of 'interfering t*ssers'! She later wrote to the school and requested that her set 2 son be moved to set 4 just so that I wouldn't be teaching him. How can you hope to build a relationship with a student who is taught to speak to teachers like that?

It is very clear who is in the wrong here! The teacher in question dealt with the situation perfectly. She stayed calm and said nothing to the parent because it was clear that she wouldn't be listened to. It's rare to encounter such an appalling example being set to a student by their own parent, and the teacher makes a very valid comment when telling her story – children learn a lot about attitudes from seeing what goes on at home and listening to what their parents or carers say. Sometimes this will cause you to feel sorry for the student, depending on circumstances, but at other times you'll be able to see just where the student gets their attitude or opinions from. So with this in mind, let's proceed to look at parents' evenings in more detail.

Parents' evenings

I have yet to meet a teacher who doesn't enjoy parents' evenings to some extent. It may not be fun having to stay until very late, but it can be wonderful to meet parents and to see the child that you teach in a very different context to that which you are used to. Hopefully you won't be nervous about meeting the parents – after all, you are still the person in a position of authority here, so don't feel intimidated. Many parents are probably dreading what might be said about their child, so they are likely to feel far more nervous than you are.

I actually love parents' evenings and am usually on quite a high afterwards! It's great to hear positive feedback from people about the work you are doing and it's also lovely to be able to give positive feedback to parents.

Look upon the evening as a chance to help better a child's education (not a chance to 'get your own back' on a challenging student), and possibly to help make your life easier. You may have a pastoral evening where you discuss your tutor group, or you may have a class or subject evening. Either way, it's around this time of year that the first parents' evenings usually occur, so here are some tips on how to get the most out of them.

Find out in advance where you'll be based

If you are a primary teacher, the chances are that you'll be based in your own room and the parents will come to you. Your evenings may take place twice a year and you may need to spread them out over more than one night.

If you are a secondary teacher, a pastoral evening may take place. Some schools only do this with Year 7 tutors, others do it across the board – in which case, you'll probably be sat as a year group, e.g. all Year 9 tutors in the gym.

Find out whether or not refreshments are served to staff beforehand

Usually in a secondary school the staff will be provided with snacks of some kind in the staffroom before the evening begins. If not, take something with you because this will be a long day.

Ask pupils for appointments well in advance

Hopefully your school provide you with a sheet on which to write down the times of your appointments. There are usually ten-minute gaps between each appointment. Ask the pupils for appointments **well in advance** unless you don't mind staying until the very end.

Note the student's name and class

If you are a secondary teacher, note down the class and name of the pupil you are seeing in the appointment space. This sounds obvious but saves confusion later and helps you to work out who is who if you don't know names yet.

Target specific students

If you want to see a specific pupil, ask them directly, don't wait for them to come to you. Many Heads of Year in secondary schools will operate a system whereby you notify them of who you wish to see. They will then ring parents to ensure that they are coming and that they are aware that a parents' evening is taking place. Some students will have been reluctant to share this information with their parents or carers!

Be prepared for disorganised students!

Some students will come to ask for an appointment roughly five minutes before the evening begins. It's up to you and your schedule as to whether or not you give them an appointment. It may be a case of saying you can ring their parents instead.

Plan appointment times

Do this carefully: it's awful to have an appointment at 5pm and no one else until 6.55pm.

Set up your space

Ensure that you have two or three chairs opposite your desk and that your room is tidy if that is where you are going to be. Some schools set up a room, such as the hall, for you. Your school should also give you a name plate to put on the desk.

Take your M&A file or make notes beforehand (or collect in their exercise books and read through them in advance)

You will know who you are going to see. If you are a primary teacher you will probably know your students very well indeed by now, certainly well enough to speak to their parents without the aid of notes. If you are a secondary teacher you may not know the kids' names yet, let alone their progress off by heart. Don't be fazed. As advised in Chapter 4, it can be a good idea to have made one note about each student when you've taken their work in, or to have noted a target about them. Take these with you and refer to them. If you haven't done so, just look through their exercise books beforehand.

If you **don't know their names**, the best thing to do is one of the following:

1 If the parent/s are not accompanied by the child, this is easy: they'll introduce themselves.
2 This has been mentioned previously and bears repeating: if the child is present, smile and ask what time their appointment was. Look quizzically at your time sheet and 'alight' upon their name as they say it, ticking it off.
3 Keep a spare of your time sheet and ask the students to tick themselves off on it.
4 Look at the parents' name tags. Most schools now give out stickers with names on as the parents come in. Often, students will be representatives of the school and they will greet the parents. Whichever tags are left over at the end of the evening represent those that did not come or turn up. However, bear in mind that many parents are remarried and so do not necessarily have the same name as their child.
5 Use your laptop – do you have a system with class names and photos on it?

I was once incredibly embarrassed to have used the wrong name for a female student the whole way through the consultation with her mother. The worst thing was that they didn't even correct me. I only realised afterwards. I had given out the wrong assessment grade, I had called her by name several times. It was awful. I began to wonder if I had gotten away with it until a couple of weeks later when I moved the class seating plan around. The girl came up to me and said, 'Perhaps you'll get to know our names now, Miss.' I cringe whenever I think of it!

Meet and greet

It's probably best to stand up behind your desk, smile and shake hands, even though you are likely to be shattered. Introduce yourself and sit back down, ready for business.

Begin by asking the student to speak

If the child is present, the best way to begin is probably to ask them how **they** think they've been doing. You can then keep a tally of how many hang their head in a hitherto unknown display of shyness and reply meekly, 'OK I s'pose.' This is probably going to be the quietest you see the student. The presence of a parent has an astounding effect!

> **tip** **Do be *honest*. It can be so easy when faced with a lovely parent to try and just paper over everything and keep smiling – but this is your chance to make a difference for the child in question and for your lessons. Be polite but be truthful.**

Alternatively, if the student is not present, get straight on with the job at hand. Tell the parent what you have been studying during lessons and then give the positives about their child. This is the same rule as with marking: start on a good note. Then slip in the targets. You will be amazed at how responsive most parents are. Point out room for improvement, end on a positive again, and then ask the parent if they have any questions.

Stick to your appointment times

Many teachers run late on parents' evenings. Try your hardest not to. It's easy to get side-tracked, but stick to the point and get the parents to do the same. At the end of the consultation, stand up and shake hands again.

Deflect complaints

If a parent has a true complaint, then the person that they need to see is not you – it is the HoD, the HoY or SLT. Direct them that way. Do so politely but firmly. You can also make use of the SENCO in this way. If a parent is being difficult, **do not be**

intimidated. Remember that you are a professional and that you know what you are talking about. Use the people around you who are there to deal with the complaints and send the parent on.

During my first subject-related parents' evening I saw the mother of a boy in my tutor group. He was there and I praised him accordingly. His mother, however, only wanted to know about his English lessons – and I don't teach English. She went off on one about how he was in set 3 for English and even stood up looking down at me over the desk. The boy looked mortified. I explained calmly that I didn't teach it, it had nothing to do with me, and I told her who to speak to. Eventually she moved on. I felt more sorry for the student than I did for myself – how embarrassing for him.

The chances are that by the time you have seen two sets of parents, you'll be well in the swing of things. You know what you are talking about and you'll get into a certain rhythm. It's a bit like writing reports in the sense that you come up with stock phrases and a set pattern to follow. With any luck you'll enjoy the experience and find that these evenings usually pass far more quickly than you imagine they will. It's always interesting to note who doesn't come to parents' evenings despite phone calls home to remind them. You can take an educated guess at this before the evening itself, and it's always sad to see those guesses become reality. These evenings can keep a parent in touch with their child – if that parent wishes to be in touch with them.

Keeping a check on your health – and how to set cover work

You'll most likely have noticed by now what a germ factory schools can be. When you think about the number of viruses that

> **tip** Remember that if you have a lot of time off in your NQT year you may need to repeat parts of it or extend it. Your mentor can advise you about this.

are floating around and the level of the heating systems in some schools – and then consider just how many little hands have grabbed that banister/textbook/biro – it's a wonder that teachers are not ill all of the time. The reason for this is that we build up an immune system. Unfortunately you do a lot of that building in your NQT year, so now is the time that you may find yourself flagging a little. If the sheer hard work and exhaustion is not enough to get you, you may find that the flu or a norovirus is. In which case:

Call in sick!

This is easier said than done. You will feel guilty, you will feel as if other people will believe that you are skiving, and you may feel as if you are lumbering your colleagues with covering you. The latter is probably true, that's the nature of the job, but at some point you'll have to cover them, so it's tough luck for now. Teaching is a truly hideous ordeal if you are unwell. The thought of a heavy cold and a thumping headache accompanying your worst-behaved students should be enough to convince you to ring your school, set your cover and then hide under the duvet. If you insist on going in the chances are you'll end up coming back home – as well as spreading your germs and becoming so poorly that you'll need even more time off anyway. These are the general rules regarding ringing in sick, guarding your health and setting cover work:

1 Don't exhaust yourself during the term. Try to maintain a distance from obviously poorly students. Wash your hands vigorously.

2. If you are ill, give in to it. You'll have guidance on ringing in sick (usually in your staff handbook). Normally you'll be expected to do so as early as possible and there is likely to be a special phone number with an answer machine dedicated to this cause.
3. Once you've rung in, **sort cover**. Email it. You don't need to worry about who will cover you – that's sorted by school. **Leave easy cover work: no class will work properly without you anyway, and no teacher who is using their non-contact to cover you wants to actually teach!** Use textbooks or worksheets. If you can't, then email your HoD asking them to do so – it is part and parcel of their job. Generally, though, be in a position to set it yourself. You don't want to be too much of an inconvenience.
4. If you are going to be off for longer than a couple of days, be advised that any longer than five days and you're going to need a sick note from a doctor.
5. Don't go back until you're better, no matter how guilty you feel. You need to recover fully.
6. Once you're back, set yourself some easy lessons for a day or so. Ease back in.

tip **When leaving cover work try to leave extension tasks too for the students who finish what you set them. This makes life easier for the cover teacher.**

These rules for setting cover do apply generally as well. If you know that you'll be off, most schools have a system you need to use. This will include leaving a sheet stuck to your desk with cover on it for each class or each part of the day. Be thorough and leave resources that are needed within easy reach. Label them with Post-it notes or something similar so that each teacher knows what is needed and when. State on your cover sheet whether you want the resources to be collected back in – if so, then where should they be left? If the TV needs to be used, then be considerate and leave instructions as to how to use it. People will appreciate this very much indeed: there is nothing worse than a teacher who knows that they'll be off and leaves no cover work. At the end of the day you cannot help it if you are unwell or away, but you can help the day to run more smoothly in your absence.

A cover work checklist

1 Have I left the cover sheet in a highly visible place?
2 Have I left enough work for each lesson or do I need extension tasks?
3 Have I clearly labelled resources for each class?
4 Have I left clear instructions for using any IT equipment in my absence?
5 Have I made a clear note of who to see if there is a problem in my absence?
6 Have I left a class list for the cover teacher?
7 Have I made it clear where to leave the resources afterwards?
8 Have I written a 'Thank You' at the bottom of my cover sheet?

Hopefully you will find yourself having a relatively healthy term and you will be able to look forward to Christmas and prepare yourself for a well-deserved break. If there is ever a holiday during which no teacher should go into school to work, it's the Christmas holiday! Whatever your religious beliefs, make the most of the entitlement to a good rest.

Some festive ideas for the final weeks of term

'Tis the season to be jolly, so (as long as it doesn't jar with any of your personal beliefs) use the excuse to spread a little festive cheer throughout your lessons and the staffroom:

If the kids give you cards, pin them up and show that they're appreciated!

Do give a Christmas card to each of your *tutor group*. You can even take a photo of them and make the cards. One primary teacher bought inexpensive Perspex baubles and decorated them with the name of the student, the class they were in and the year. (Your year group budget can cover the cost of the baubles.)

If your school or year group do not already have a '*post-box*' service for the students to post their Christmas cards in, organise one. You can nominate members of each tutor group or class to make 'deliveries' via the National Elf Service.

***Secret Santa* is always a good idea – the ICT teachers at one secondary school organise this each year. Each member of staff fills in a form about their likes and dislikes and hands it in. The names are then distributed with a £10 cash limit for presents. One small gift is given each day of the last week of term and placed in the appropriate pigeonhole.**

Decorate your classroom for Christmas. See if you can organise an inter-tutor group or year group competition for best-dressed classroom. If you're a secondary teacher you can get the kids to take the decorations down on the last day. If you're primary, you can do it yourself just after the students leave on the last day.

Make sure that you give some chocolates or another token of esteem to your *mentor* – you may actively wish to do so or you may think that they are entirely undeserving, but it's still a good idea to thank them for giving up their time to do your paperwork and so on.

Do the staff at your school give out *Christmas cards* to one another? In one school, the teachers all write one card to the staff as a whole. They pin it on a noticeboard and give the cash that they'd have spent otherwise to a collection for a local children's hospice. If confident enough, you could suggest or organise this.

Have a rest! That's your first term done, you're a third of the way there. The last week or so before Christmas is always fun in school, whether you're primary or secondary, so wind down and start to relax. Enjoy your time off and come back refreshed in the New Year.

If given the chance to have *Christmas lunch* with the kids, then do so – they love to see their teachers at events like this and all these little things help to build your relationships with them.

If you're a primary teacher with a *Christmas tree* up in your room hang a tree chocolate up for each child and allow them one by one to find their own before they leave on the last day of term.

Chapter 7

And onwards to summer

In this chapter you will find advice that should see you through to the end of the summer term. This period of time will go surprisingly quickly, and before you know it you'll have completed (and passed!) your NQT year. It's also a time for reflection, and in the following chapter we will consider the importance of this as you enter your second year. For now, though, you can find advice on the following:

- Writing reports
- The options process
- The build-up to exams (GCSEs, SATs and so on)
- Evaluating your NQT year
- What to do if there is a problem

After Christmas, you may notice a sharp difference in your relationship with the students. You will have been away on your first 'holiday' period and come back not as a new teacher, but as a teacher that they are accustomed to seeing about the place. The same goes for other members of staff. You'll be recognised and will be 'part of the furniture'. This can be massively reassuring because you'll notice that even the students who were 'testing' you at first will no longer see any novelty in this, and instead they will know where they stand with you. You'll have more influence and a greater presence in the school. An excellent boost for your confidence!

tip This is a good time of year to ensure that you tackle any remaining class management issues. If you have problems with a particular class then make sure you face them head-on: ask your mentor and any other experienced teachers for advice. Go to observe them being taught by other teachers if possible and continue to work on strategies.

Writing reports

Unless you have had to write a tutor report of any kind before Christmas (and these are usually very brief) your first experience of writing any form of report may come around now. Primary teachers will usually write an average of two reports a year, and secondary teachers will usually write one subject report per student per year. You may also have to write a pastoral comment about the student, depending on whether or not you have a tutor group. The following checklist is useful for organising yourself when it comes to reports because they can constitute a lot of work that needs to be squeezed in to an already hectic schedule.

Report checklist

1 Know well in advance when the reports are due.

This should be in your calendar or handbook and you should be aware that different schools have different names for them, e.g. Progress reviews, RoA (Record of Achievement) and so on.

2 Plan a timetable for writing them.

Work out which students or classes you are going to write first and in which order. You may prefer to group ability together or just plough through the register. Everyone has their own system or style.

3 If you share a class, ensure that you discuss who will be writing the reports.

You may each write one or you may divide the class up.

4 Check on the format of the reports.

Some schools still handwrite reports, others use an online system. Find out how to use the system in advance and ensure that you **save work as you go** – it's very frustrating to lose everything you've done!

5 Is there a word count?

It can be very irritating to be bound by a word count because you may feel that you need more space to write a meaningful and worthwhile report. However, there is little you can do about this other than make the most of parents' evenings and phone calls home (positive as well as negative) to relay information.

6 Use a comment bank...

You will automatically build up your own comment bank in your head and you can save time if you use IT generated reports by typing up your own. Other schools may have comment banks pre-prepared for you to use.

7 But beware of copy and paste!

If you do use a comment bank, be sure to still make your reports individual to the student! Beware of pasting 'he' when you mean 'she'! Chances are they will be proofread by an office or an HoD anyway and some schools will ask you to rewrite them if they are blatant copy and pastes.

8 Use your M&A file and exercise books.

Use all the tools at your disposal to ensure that you do justice to the student and their progress. If you cannot picture who a student is, look up their photo in the school mugshot book or online system.

9 Start on a positive.

Try to follow the advice for marking work: start on a positive, write a target, end on a positive.

10 Aim it at the parent.

The person you are writing to is the parent and not the student, so aim it at them.

11 Hand them in on time!

Many teachers hand reports in late and this can be infuriating – particularly if you are a tutor and need the entire report before making your pastoral comment. As with all aspects of teaching, be professional and considerate and think of your reputation.

12 Plug your subject.

If you are a secondary teacher with Year 9 classes, you may wish to consider a little subject marketing here. In other words, if you have a student who you believe will do very well at GCSE, then say so now. This is your chance!

The purpose of reports

As with parents' evenings, the purpose of a report is to point out what a student is doing well and what they need to improve – not to get your own back on a kid who has been driving you mad since 1 September. However, it is important to be **honest**. You need to express in no uncertain terms how a pupil is progressing and sometimes that is going to annoy a parent, especially those who believe their child is a ray of sunshine. The key is to get your message across but be polite and start and end on a positive note. Keep the tone upbeat and full of high expectation. The following tale is from a secondary teacher that had problems with a flirtatious Year 8 girl:

I was determined to get the message through to this girl's parents that their daughter was on the way to building a real reputation for herself, but I wanted to do it as appropriately as possible. The only thing she ever did in my classroom was flirt with boys – it was embarrassing to watch. I decided that this needed to go in her report and so I wrote the following:

X has demonstrated on frequent occasions this year that she is capable of hard work. However, she remains unlikely to fulfil any true potential unless she learns to restrain herself in class – I'd like to see the best of her academic ability as opposed to her ability to distract the boys. I have high expectations of her and would hate to see her waste her chances in school.

This was proofread by the HoY and the Head and no one ever commented back to me – nor did her parents, so I assume that they took it in the spirit I intended, an honest reflection on what the student needed to do to improve!

You need to keep your reports **professional and useful**. They should fulfil their purpose in that a parent can read them and see what their child does well and how they can do even better.

Areas to comment on

You'll know what you want to comment on – generally what is done well and what needs to be improved. This may include:

Concentration

Focus

Written style/arguments

Spelling/punctuation/grammar

Appropriate behaviour

Explanations

Knowledge

Thinking skills

Listening skills

Articulation

Method

Practical elements

The list could be endless, depending on the subject. Just decide which is most crucial. You don't have a huge amount of space to write in so stick to the key issue for an individual student. This may revolve around a specific assessment or recent project if this helps you to focus the report. In some schools you may need to give feedback on specific objectives.

Comments

You will have your own personal style of report writing and will know what you want to say. I've included some examples here of comments to get you thinking, but the likelihood is that once you get into the swing of writing, you'll find it comes very naturally indeed.

Comments to open with

X's progress this year has been outstanding and I have been extremely pleased with her/his progress . . .

X's progress this year has at times been very good indeed, however . . .

X has demonstrated this year that s/he is certainly capable of producing some good work. However, this has not been consistent . . .

X has shown a real improvement in recent work . . .

X's oral work in class has been very good this year, however, s/he now needs to begin . . .

Target comments

These can be used in conjunction with the 'Areas to comment on' listed above.

X can now begin to develop . . .

The key for improvement will be a consistent approach . . .

X should now endeavour to build upon this progress by . . .

I should now like to see X turn her/his attention to . . .

In order to improve even further . . .

Comments to end with

If X can do so, then I am sure that s/he will succeed.

This would be wonderful to see and I wish her/him every success in the future.

I look forward to seeing this improvement.

I have every expectation that s/he will be successful.

Very well done indeed, X! (Although you are writing to the parent, it is usually seen as fine to end on a comment that can be seen to include the student.)

These comments should give an idea of the 'tone' of a report. It should be succinct and to the point.

> **tip** If you have a child who is very disheartened by a report that a teacher has written, it can be an idea to dig out one of your own from your schooldays that you found to be disappointing. This will help to build their self-esteem and hopefully show that no one can be good at everything. I remember my own Year 9 physics report that said only the following:
> 'Verity is out of her depth in this subject.'
> Full of constructive advice, then!

Pastoral reports

The pastoral report will be written by you either as the class teacher or as the tutor, depending upon what ages you teach. There are various things you can comment on and normally these will 'round off' a report. If you have read the rest of the report that has been written by other teachers, then you can also sum up the general tone of the report and mention any main areas for improvement or commendation. I have commented on the following in the past, but there is such a broad range here. You know your students better than anyone else by now, and you will know what needs to be said.

Behaviour

Uniform

Helpfulness

Attitude

Extra-curricular activities

Manners

Sense of humour

Friendship groups

Bullying issues

Social skills

General demeanour

Time-keeping

Student self-evaluation

Many schools have a policy whereby the student will read their report before it goes home and will add their own handwritten self-evaluation of their progress. It can be useful to structure this for them to ensure that it does not read as though it is merely a box-ticking exercise. Suggest constructive comments – it is amazing how many students will simply write, 'I am pleased. My target is to work harder next year', and believe that this is enough. Think back to the ideas behind AfL (see Chapter 5) and get your students to think of smart targets for themselves that are realistic and measurable. You can use tutor or class time to do this and it is worth doing properly.

After you have completed one set of reports you will be prepared for next time in terms of what to write and how much work is required. This will make the whole process easier: you'll find yourself thinking throughout the year of things that could go in a student's report. If this is the case, you can even make a note of it in your M&A file to save time later on. If you can, then ensure that you have access to a copy of your previous report for a student, as this means that you can compare and contrast them – and that you can highlight progress more easily.

The options process

This is really only relevant for secondary school teachers, so do feel free to skip on ahead if you are a primary teacher!

> **tip** Keep info about the GCSE up on your walls – make it look exciting and refer to it all year long. Keep it there in the forefront of students' minds from Year 7 onwards.

The options process for choosing GCSE subjects actually begins for most schools around the middle of September, because as soon as the staff have settled back into the new year, they will be thinking about how best to recruit as many students as they can for the following year. In fact, many departments begin this recruiting process as early as Year 7, at least in the sense of making their subject seem as exciting and relevant as they possibly can, with references to GCSE courses being made very early on indeed. In actual fact, of course, the real recruiting begins with Year 9 just after Christmas – though many Heads of Department will encourage you to begin plugging away with Year 9 before then.

This may sound extreme to you at the moment, but you will be shocked by just how militant some departments can be! After all, the very survival of your subject in a school can depend solely on how many kids opt for it at GCSE. If you don't get enough, the GCSE may not run – and this can impact upon staffing levels. However, as an NQT you don't need to worry too much about this as it is not your sole responsibility. You'll be told nearer the time (so generally around now, after Christmas) what 'marketing strategies' will be in force in your department, and you'll be encouraged to join in.

Marketing your subject

In a sense, you will have been doing this with Year 9 since September: they'll have been thinking about what subjects to take or drop since then, and the ones that seem most relevant to them will be the ones they go for. Your teaching style, then, has a great impact here as do your resources and your relationship with the kids. However, there are certain other things that you can do and that your HoD may encourage you to do:

1 Put up posters about the GCSE in your room/the corridors etc.
2 Make a PowerPoint about the GCSE and show it to your classes.
3 Ask current enthusiastic Year 10 and 11 students to write testimonies about the GCSE.
4 Ask current Year 10 and 11 students to come and speak to Year 9.
5 Do assemblies about the GCSE.
6 Send postcards home to the students that you particularly wish to target.
7 Mention suitability for the GCSE in reports that go home or at parents' evening.
8 Highlight any exciting GCSE trips or residentials.

Bear in mind however that other departments are likely to do the same – and some can be very competitive. There will be more on the dangers of this later on.

The options evening

A huge part of the build-up to the options will be the options evening. You may not need to attend this – it is probably the responsibility of your HoD – but you may wish to go anyway. Generally, your subject teachers will have an area of their own to set up with displays and activities that are designed to draw in the students from Year 9 and their parents. You may enlist some Year 10 or 11 students to come along and speak to them as well, or you may try out your marketing patter yourself.

Overly pushy departments!

Much as I enjoy promoting my subject at this time of year – and it is certainly a high when you get a lot of students taking your GCSE – I am also wary of it. Four things seem to get missed at this time of year, and they are all crucial:

1 **Students should not take a subejct just because their parents or carers went them to.**
2 **Students should not take a subject because *you* want them to.**
3 **Students should not take a subject because they think you'll be teaching them.**
4 **Students should not take a subject because their friends are taking it.**

Some departments and teachers seem to forget that these are the students' choices and that they are about the students' futures. The following is an example of what can happen in some schools when the teachers forget this:

I had a Year 9 tutor group and one very sweet boy was really upset about the options. He had literally taken as much as he could of pushy teachers. One day, he received a letter at home from the music department saying that the teachers were looking forward to seeing his parents at the options evening and discussing his choice to take music. He had no intention of taking it and didn't have a musical bone in his body – but the department sent these to every child just to draw their parents in to the process and add more pressure. Totally unfair! Some of the kids felt that this was just too much and were very upset by it – they were bombarded from all subject directions.

It is crucial not to get caught up in this kind of departmental crossfire. It is unfair to the students and it really does them an injustice. Instead, I tend to reiterate the four highlighted points above. Students need to consider what they want to do after school and think about what will help them and what they enjoy. They need to be totally selfish and very mature in their choices – and if they really want to take your subject, then they will. They will see that you are respecting their freedom of choice here and, in turn, they will respect you for that.

'Pathways' – are they really 'options'?

Most schools now operate a kind of 'Pathways' system for GCSE choices. This means that different students will be catered for with different courses. For example, a school may link up with a nearby college which can provide vocational options or courses such as construction. However, depending on the school that you work in, these may either be advised as the best route for a student or they may be 'suggested' in a far more pressurised manner.

An example of the latter would be where a school produces three different-coloured sheets of 'options', such as yellow, pink and green. Each of these would list different courses: the yellow may have all academic subjects, the pink may have a mixture of academic and vocational, and the green may have only vocational courses. The Year 7 CAT test results of the students will then be examined. Depending on what those results were, the students will then be given a yellow, a pink or a green sheet. They can therefore only 'choose' from what is on the sheet.

The problem with this, of course, is that students are individuals. I have taught very low-ability kids who happen to be G&T (gifted and talented) in my subject – and who have come out of the GCSE with an excellent grade. Had I taught these students in a school that follows the above example of coloured Pathways, those students would automatically have been relegated to a pink or green sheet – neither of which even gives the choice of a humanities GCSE. It is for you to decide what your own opinions about this method are, but it is a contentious issue in some schools at the moment. The following examples are from two different schools:

Our Pathways system is very fair – the Year 9 tutors spend a lot of time with the kids and help them decide what they want to do and how best to get qualified. They think about where the kids' skills lie and go from there. The students are able then to pick whatever they are most suited to and what is best for them. This can include more traditional subjects as well because a child who doesn't succeed in maths may excel in philosophy. Our results are very good – an average of a 75% pass rate over the last five years. The students still have the choice therefore, but they are encouraged to think carefully before making it.

I can't help but think that we railroad kids into making choices. In fact, there is no 'choice'. I remember a parent telling me that you can't choose fish and chips if it's not on the menu, and that's the case with our coloured Pathways. Even if the parents complain and the student gets to take whatever subject they wanted to, that child has still had their coloured sheet handed out to them. It's like they've been branded by it in front of all their mates. I don't think it's good for their self-esteem.

Whatever your school policy and whatever your views, in the end just do your best by the kids. That's what we're there for, and the students always appreciate the teachers who put them first.

The build-up to exams

It is of course at around this time that a great many exams will be taking place. This can be nerve-racking because part of the responsibility for results lies with you for your classes. However, it can also be great, because if you are a secondary school teacher your Year 11 time is now free once they have left. You should no longer have to invigilate external exams (praise be because this is a mind-numbing task) and therefore you can relax a little. The following is a list of external exams in both primary and secondary schools:

tip **It can be a nice idea to make tiny good luck cards for your students. You should save time by using ICT and just printing these off, but it can boost their morale during your final lesson with them before the exams.**

Year 2: SATs

Year 6: SATs

Year 7: CATs

Year 9: SATs

Year 10/11: GCSEs (Some modules to be sat in Year 10)

Year 12: AS Levels

Year 13: A2 Levels

The build-up to these can be tense for everyone – but at least if you have already faced the mocks then you know where your students stand and what you have needed to do for them during the past four or five months to get them up to scratch. Look back over the advice from Chapter 6 if necessary and then relax a little. In the end, however much work you have put in the students need to do the same. You can't sit the exam for them and you can't do their revision. Make the most of any extra free time that you now have and use it wisely. However, if you are starting to feel summer term fatigue around now, take it easy. Not long to go and you will have six weeks of R&R to look forward to!

Tips for preparing students

- Go over the past papers.
- Make revision cards.

- Hold after-school (or lunchtime) revision sessions. Advertise these around the school. Provide chocolate!
- Use websites such as GCSE Bitesize (see Chapter 10 for more websites).
- Make revision games or quizzes.
- Go through the students' targets and see if they have been achieved.
- Practise exam style and timings.
- Remind students of what they can take into the exam.
- Ensure that the students know how many questions to answer and so on.
- Go to the start of the exam if you can, just to show you care.

Do remember that if you are a secondary school teacher you can go into school in the third week of August when the results come out and celebrate with your students! This can be a great feeling, and they will really enjoy seeing you and telling you what grades they have achieved. It also means that you can congratulate yourself on a job well done.

Year 6/11/13 leavers

It is at this time of year that you are going to lose some students: you may be very glad to see the back of a couple of them, but you are likely to feel pretty sad about others going. The fun thing is that they will probably have a leavers' do or prom of some kind – and that you will get to go along and join in the fun. This is a great opportunity, so take it if you get the chance. It's fantastic to see the students in a different light, and they will enjoy seeing you there. At one school where I have taught, the teachers actually serve the meal to the students before the music starts later in the evening. There is a real sense of tradition and pride. The following tales are from two different schools (and they clearly have very different students!).

The leavers' do at my school was really emotional! I just kept welling up and had to choke back the tears, which took me by surprise. My tutor group had been Year 11 and seeing them all dressed up was fantastic. They arrived outside the school in a great variety of vehicles – fire engines, vintage cars, even a bed with a motor attached! The whole town turned out to see them. It was an amazing experience and such a rite of passage for them. I felt indescribably proud.

Our Year 11 spent their last day in school and I couldn't understand beforehand why the SLT kept the leaving date a secret. They only told the kids the previous day. It turns out that it's because the students wreak havoc! They sprayed so much graffiti over the back of the school that a company had to be called in by lunchtime to remove it all (at a huge cost) and they lit flares and disposable BBQs on the field. A couple had to be arrested and some even put bleach all over the toilet seats. The worst part, though, was about four weeks after they had left. A Year 9 girl suddenly realised that maggots were falling on her head from the ceiling tiles in her English classroom – which explained where the rotten fish smell had been coming from for the last month!

Presumably, if you have a Year 6 group that are leaving, then you will be spared the usual egg-and-flour throwing contests that are so enjoyed by the older kids!

Evaluating your NQT year

So here you are: a whole year will have flown by in a blur of teaching, report writing and various open evenings. A few weeks and you will be off for the summer and – you'll have passed the year with flying colours! It's great to know that you're off 'probation', and that when you come back in September you will no longer be under the mentorship of anyone, probably for the first time since you began training. You've done it – **congratulations!**

The speed at which the academic year passes can be frightening. If you think back to a year ago you were most probably wondering what on earth to prepare over the summer, and you may be thinking the same this year. However, it's really the same advice: just try to relax. At least this time you will go back knowing exactly what you'll be teaching – and if you are desperate to do at least a modicum of preparation, the following is an 'If you really must' list.

If you really must prepare for September:

- Sort your room out either before breaking up or over the summer. Check school opening times: most have building work over the summer.
- Sort your photocopying for the first couple of days back just so that you are off to a running start and you don't swamp the reprographics department come September.
- Check the date you are due back and whether it will be INSET or not. Do you need to sign up now for lunch if it is INSET?
- Fill your new planner (school should have given you a new one by now) with dates from the new calendar.
- Check your class lists and ensure you have your timetable.
- RELAX!

That really is about it – but then you'll know that yourself by now!

So how have you done?

I've spoken before about the importance of self-evaluation, and you'll have been taking part in a steady process of this throughout the year, especially during your induction sessions. It is pretty amazing to look back over the year and to see how far you have come – even if you were a very good trainee teacher, it doesn't really compare to how good you can be once your NQT year is over. We tend to underestimate just how much we will develop over the course of the induction year, and it is only when we reflect back on it that we come to realise what a transition has taken place.

You will have learnt a variety of lessons yourself over the year, from how to interact with SLT to how to defuse a fight in the playground. It is important now to look back with a critical eye and to decide what areas you wish to focus on next year. Ask yourself the following questions:

Focus	Target and/or strategy
What part of my professional development have I been most proud of over the year?	e.g. Developing an excellent relationship with a very challenging class and modifying my planning and differentiation in order to give them the best chance of learning and succeeding. The class were empowered and developed their self-esteem. Target: Feel confident to do the same where necessary with next year's classes and have patience (without feeling defeated!) if we do not 'click' immediately – I know now that it can take time!
Which areas of my class management have been especially good – and where is there further room for improvement?	e.g. My consistent approach to classroom rules – although this did take time to develop. Target: Begin September in the same vein, with more confidence than last year, knowing that I am in control.

How well do I feel I have managed my time?	*e.g. Very well: I settled into a rhythm very quickly once the term got under way.*
Am I pleased with how my relationship with the students has progressed? Do I create a safe and secure learning environment?	*e.g. Students felt comfortable discussing contentious issues and became accustomed to speaking their mind and listening to others: a sure sign that they felt comfortable in class. They knew where boundaries lay and respected those so I am very pleased with this.*
Is there any one particular area that I clearly need to focus on next year?	*e.g. I'd still like to focus on class management as an ongoing target. Every class is different so I would never become complacent. I look forward to the challenge!*

This should help to provide a clear focus for you, and it will also help you in September when it comes to reviewing and renewing your Performance Management Review from last year. The best teachers are those who continually reflect upon their practice and learn from their own performance, taking on board advice from others where needed. It is only through sharing

tip **Keep an eye out for any training courses that you can go on – your HoD should get info about them or there will be a person in school who can help you. Once you know which areas you'd like to focus on in your next year, take every chance you can to develop your career profile.**

best practice that we can hope to be outstanding teachers – thereby giving our students outstanding opportunities in their education.

What to do if there is a problem

Hopefully you are only reading this section out of interest, but if you are not, and there is indeed a problem, then take heart in the fact that you will not be alone.

Teaching is an incredibly demanding job: it makes demands on our time, our social life, our bodies and our minds. Every other job in the world begins with teaching of some kind, and this is often overlooked by people outside the profession. It also means that stress is rife in teaching – and if you do not enjoy the work to start with, this only makes things worse. I have often thought that it must be terrible to be stuck in a teaching job if you do not love it. There is a big difference between having a moan in the staffroom at break time and going home in tears at the end of the day because you loathe it all so much. If the latter applies to you, it's not the end of the world – it just means that this is not the right career for you, and that another one will be. It doesn't mean either that you can't work with kids or young people, it is simply that teaching is not the way to do it.

If you do find yourself in the position of being very unhappy, then think **very carefully** about whether it is definitely because of the job, and whether or not there is anything that will make it better. Speak to other NQTs, speak to your friends and family, and speak to your mentor if you feel that you can trust them. The first few years of teaching are always the hardest, but you shouldn't be feeling thoroughly miserable.

Generally, you will know if it is not for you. If you are not cut out to teach, then no matter what school you work in or who you work with, you will not enjoy it – and there is no way around that. If this turns out to be the case, don't worry about what other people may think; make your decision and take it from there. It doesn't mean, of course, that you have to give up teaching for ever. The following tale is from a music teacher:

I taught for four years and towards the end of the fourth year decided that I needed a break from it all. I had problems with the SLT in my school but also fancied some time away. I applied for a job with an old boss of mine and I got it. I fully intend to return to teaching when the time is right – but I have to admit that in the meantime I REALLY miss the holidays!

Do bear in mind that if you are unhappy because of a particular situation in school, then you can and should make the most of your union representative. You can find more information about union representatives in Chapter 3.

The summer – it's here at last! Six weeks of social life and relaxation! Make the most of it – you have well and truly earned it. **Well done**.

Chapter 8

Your second year and beyond

You will probably notice a huge difference between starting at your school last September and going back this September. For starters, you are now part of the furniture – but also, your class management may be considerably different simply because your confidence will have increased tenfold.

This chapter gives advice about the following:

- Self-evaluation, improvement and training
- Career progression
- Class management in your second September
- Ofsted
- Having a family and juggling your 'work/life balance'

Self-evaluation, improvement and training

As was mentioned at the end of the previous chapter, it is incredibly important that you now begin to evaluate your practice and to decide how you are going to develop and continue improving and learning. The best way to do this is to set your aims and then think of specific ways in which to tackle them.

tip Any new academic year can be daunting but this time you know what to expect. This is the time of year where you can begin to take on a couple of extra responsibilities or join a working party to raise your profile a bit. Don't take on too much, though!

Take any opportunity you get to attend **training courses**. Some schools are very good about sending teachers on courses, but others are not. Often this is down to budget restraints. However, you should be offered the opportunity to go on a course at least once a year, so if you can, then sign up as soon as possible. Try to pick something practical that will benefit you directly, but even if you end up on a course that isn't of specific interest to you, at least you know that you can include it in your portfolio as training you have received.

Many schools will actually provide training on **INSET days** (after all, that's what they are for), so you can benefit sometimes from signing up to various courses in-school. Teachers often specialise in an area, such as thinking skills or SEN, and can then share their expertise with the rest of the staff. If this is the case, it may be worth finding out who specialises in which area – you can always arrange to meet them after school or observe one of their lessons if it is an area that interests you. Even finding out which teachers are technical whizz-kids on the interactive whiteboards can be beneficial because they can share advice with you. And, who knows: you may well have something to share with them. Make the most of the experienced staff that you have readily available on site.

Keep a note and **evidence of any training** you receive. If you attend a course, you'll usually be given some form of paper evidence, and this can go in a portfolio. The chances are that you may never have to show that to anyone at a job interview, but it's wise to be prepared.

tip Keep an eye out for NQTs starting this year. Join a new staff buddy system if your school has one and make them feel welcome. It's great to share experiences and you'll still be in the position of remembering what it's like to be new.

Career progression

The purpose of all of this training is not only to develop yourself to the best of your ability, but also to aid career progression. Whether you want to remain a classroom teacher or if you want to shoot straight for the heady heights of SLT, you have to stay on top of your game.

It is usually seen as a wise move to stay in your first school for around four or five years. (This may not always be possible, of course, due to factors outside or inside the school, so do not worry if you have to move on beforehand.) This gives you time to begin proving yourself and your capabilities and also to settle for a while and decide what you would like to do. Depending on whether you are a primary or a secondary teacher, different options apply. You can go for these opportunities internally or you can apply externally when you feel ready. Remember that it can be easier to get a job as an internal candidate. Many teachers experience a sense of doom when going to an interview and finding that one or two internal applicants are present. You clearly have a distinct advantage if you already work there because, however impartial the process, the school do know you.

The kinds of position that you may find yourself being able to apply for are as follows:

- Curriculum leader (especially in primary school, where you may be a leader for PE and ICT, for example)
- Assistant Head of Year (in a smaller school this may not be a paid position but is great experience)
- Head of Year
- Second in Department
- Head of Department (or Lead Practitioner)
- Professional tutor (the one who takes care of the university trainees)
- AST (Advanced Skills Teacher: you need your Head's backing and will have to check this out with the LEA to check on funding first, unless your school will fund you)
- Head of Faculty
- SLT

This is actually a pretty basic list of positions. As you'll know, depending on what school you work in there are innumerable titles and vacancies that come up in middle management. Some schools may have a Lead Practitioner who is essentially the HoD. However, they may have another member of staff in that department who is **also** an LP, just with different responsibilities. If you work in a foundation school, for example, your internal structure may vary radically from that in a school that is LEA-funded.

It may seem rather ambitious to even consider applying for an HoD job in your early years of teaching, but some teachers become HoD in their **NQT year**: you may get thrown in at the deep end but you'll certainly have earned your wages by the end of the month! SLT obviously takes more time, and generally so would an HoY position, but there is no reason not to apply for an HoD or subject leader post if you know your stuff and the opportunity arises.

One thing that is certainly true is that if you are a male primary teacher, you can expect your career to progress rapidly should you so wish. This is a blatant form of positive discrimination, but it's often the case. You can start aiming for assistant headships (and be successful in landing one) very early on – particularly in comparison with those male teachers who work in secondary schools.

Whatever you decide to do and however you wish to go about progressing: **be sensible**. Apply for positions once you are ready – do not leave a school you love just because you're impatient to prove yourself. You'll know when you are ready to move on, but bear the following tales in mind:

I stayed at my last school for far too long. It became stale and had a detrimental effect on my teaching. I knew that the time had come to move on and I should have been brave enough to do so, but I stuck around. This soured my memories of the place. – A Deputy Head in a secondary school

---

I left my first school too quickly! I went to an HoD post after four years of teaching, and although I was more than ready professionally, I should have taken my time. I applied for the first thing that came up and bitterly regretted it. I hadn't researched the school that I moved to and I was heartbroken. My first school was lovely, and I suddenly realised that I'd only been teaching for *four years* – that's nothing! I could have stayed and taken my time and been happy. I wish that I had. I was just too impatient.

Bide your time and think carefully, and then – if you're still sure it's the right move for you – **go for it**. (Just reread the jobs info in Chapter 1 first!)

Class management

> **tip** As with your NQT year, make the most of the first couple of weeks as far as class managment goes – get on top of it now whilst the idea of being back at school is still a novelty for the kids. Remember that they'll be reasonably quiet at this stage, so make your mark and start as you mean to go on.

While we are on the subject of career progression, a quick word about class management. You are likely to be **much more stringent** about your class management this year. Even if you were very much on top of things last year, your new confidence around the place will help to make you an even better teacher. Three things contribute to this:

1. You know the kids.
2. The kids know you.
3. You know the system and the school itself.

Subsequently, you know that you don't have to take any bad behaviour in your room, and you know that even if it takes time, you can develop different approaches until you find the one that works. The sense of panic that we sometimes feel when we are new to teaching begins to disappear. Some behaviour can be curbed overnight – little misdemeanours and so forth – but other things do and will take time. And you have all year. So, don't panic if the kids don't all behave like angels from the beginning of September onwards, but do allow yourself to feel rather pleased that many will simply behave well because they know you now and they know your expectations. They won't have forgotten them over the summer.

Ofsted

Aaah, Ofsted! You may have experience of Ofsted already, you may even have been observed by them during training, but your second year seems as good a time as any to give them a little mention. (It is also important to mention that Ofsted does not exist in Wales – instead inspections are carried out by ESTYN.)

Ofsted and the inspection process have changed considerably in the last four years. Gone are the days when a school had several weeks' notice prior to a visit. Gone also are the times where the inspectors spent a week in school with you and there were too many of them to count. Instead, emphasis is now placed upon self-evaluation (there is some information about this and your school's SEF in Chapter 5), and you are likely to have approximately two or three days' notice of a visit. There will only be a couple of inspectors and this should be a little less daunting than the old routine. Your Head will have been updating a SEF throughout the year and Ofsted will come to check that the school is on track and that your Head knows their school. The leader of a school needs to know what is being done well and what needs to be improved, and Ofsted will judge this for themselves.

I am the kind of sad individual who actually enjoys being observed, but then I also quite liked exams at school. However, this wasn't because I was a great brainiac (I was not – see my physics report in Chapter 7), it was simply because I made sure that I **prepared**. The same with Ofsted: unless you have a TLR for something, you can expect to be observed but you won't be in the position of justifying results and so on to anyone. In fact, it's possible that you may not even be observed (especially if you work in a huge secondary school), but it's best to be ready. Think of it as a chance to show off your marvellous teaching skills – you've been observed hundreds of times before, and this is no different.

The running of an inspection usually goes along these lines:

- Ofsted arrive and you meet the inspectors.
- They do their stuff and observe different lessons and decide who they would like to see and who they would like to speak to. You should be given a timetable of this so that you know what is going on.
- Ofsted stay for a couple of days and on the final day feedback to the Head.
- The Head feeds back to the staff once the inspection is over.
- You will get a written report. No one but the Head will be named in this.
- The students will be given a letter from Ofsted that thanks them and points out the main findings.

The Ofsted report used to be many pages long but it is now much shorter. The inspection grades have also changed along with the inspection process, and are now as follows –

tip If you have an inspection and something that you have done in school is favourably highlighted in the report, then pop it in your portfolio. You won't be named, but you should still claim the credit for your hard work!

Grade 1: Outstanding

Grade 2: Good

Grade 3: Satisfactory

Grade 4: Inadequate

There is quite a leap here between being judged 'good' and being judged 'outstanding'. The grade 'very good' no longer exists in Ofsted speak, and some teachers that I have spoken to would rather that it did.

The report itself will be broken down into key areas that will be commented on and graded according to this scale. These areas are as follows:

Introduction	This will include the number of inspectors who carried out the visit.
Description of the school	Is the school over- or undersubscribed? What proportion have SEN or free school meals and so on?
Key for inspection grades	As above.
Overall effectiveness of the school	A fairly detailed report about the school overall, including a grade.
Effectiveness of different stages: for example, in primary, the Foundation Stage	This will include a grade and comments about what the school can do to improve further.
Achievement and standards	Is the progression of pupils tracked efficiently and is this tracking used to promote further learning? What achievements really stand out in the school? A grade will be given.
Personal development and well-being	Spiritual, moral, social and cultural development will be commented on and a grade will be given.
'Quality of provision' is then reported on and will include the following areas **Teaching and learning** **Curriculum and other activities** **Care, guidance and support** **Leadership and management**	Comments and grades will be given for each of these subheadings.

Inspection judgements	These will be given in table format and will break down the areas. For example, personal development and well-being may include 'how well learners enjoy their education' and this will be given a grade.

If you do happen to be observed during an inspection – and it used to be that all teachers would be observed approximately three times during the visit – you can expect to be told the grade of your lesson and the reasons for this. Remember, however, that depending on the size of your school, you may not be seen.

It is always interesting to see the effect that an imminent inspection has upon a school. Part of the thinking behind having only a couple of days' notice is that teachers will not have to prepare so much paperwork in advance or get in such a flap about the visit. Your Head will already have a pretty good idea of when the inspection will take place anyway, and the idea is that you should always be performing to the level at which Ofsted find you. The inspectors are not there to catch you out – they are there to help. However, most schools and most departments go a bit bonkers before a visit, tidying, typing, planning and photocopying evidence. The most important thing for you to do though is to **plan your lessons**. As long as you have done this, you have nothing to worry about. So, should an inspector call, good luck and try to enjoy the experience! At the very least the whole school will be clubbing together in a kind of war effort with a Blitz mentality, so you can make the most of that and support each other.

Having a family and juggling your work/life balance

Whilst speaking to many teachers during the research of this book, the issue of work/life balance was one that came up in conversation time and time again. This is always tricky when teaching. You may well already have a family before you even go into the profession – in which case you know the struggles that this issue can cause – but if you are planning to have one, then try not to get stressed about the impact of work on your outside life. By now you are well into the swing of things, and it is safe to say that you will simply find another rhythm much as you had to when you first started teaching.

The general advice from various male and female teachers, is to stay organised – but to ensure that your family are your priority, no matter how work may feel about that. If your kids are sick, you ring in and you set cover. **Do not feel guilty**. The following are different examples from men and women who teach in both primary and secondary schools:

In my school I asked the Head of Faculty what to do if I wanted to go to one of my daughters' Christmas plays or productions. He basically said that I should ring in sick, because the Head here won't allow time off for that. He's pretty good if your kids are poorly, but attending sporting events and so on is not seen as a priority.

I've noticed a stark difference between my old Head, who was male, and my new Head, who is female. She is far more understanding of family commitments. When my wife was first pregnant, my old Head even suggested that I not take all of my paternity leave. You can imagine how my wife and I felt about that suggestion! The new Head is far more accommodating and has a young family herself.

My daughter had chickenpox and my husband and I had to juggle the week, each taking a couple of days off. We worked it around meetings that we had in school and other commitments, so made the effort to ensure that we could attend the 'essentials'. Both of our Heads seemed to appreciate this and were fine about our respective absences.

I remember when my daughter was only a year old and poorly with a sickness bug. My mother had her on the Monday and my husband was taking Tuesday and Wednesday off. I asked the Head if I could take Thursday and Friday and was appalled when he replied, 'Can't you juggle the week with your husband?' I pointed out that unless I was doing that already, I wouldn't be in school, would I? He relented and agreed but I was furious afterwards!

My Head has always been very lenient when it comes to family commitments. He seems to work on the basis that if you treat your staff fairly and with respect, then they will do the same for you. And of course, he's right. No one takes advantage, but if you need the time off and you need it legitimately, he's happy to help you.

The vast majority of schools are filled with working parents: you won't be alone in needing to balance your life carefully, whether you are male or female.

Pregnancy

> **website**
> Check out the following website for your maternity and paternity rights: **www.direct.gov.uk**

If you are female and you are planning a pregnancy, then in terms of pay increases and promotions, you can expect to be treated fairly and in the same manner as anyone else who is not pregnant. Most schools and Heads have a lot of experience in dealing with pregnant members of staff and you can speak to the school finance officer about your leave entitlements and any packages that your LEA offer. Whether or not you are entitled to a package depends on your length of continuous service and you can check with the LEA. Your entitlement as far as statutory pay, however, is the same wherever you work, so have a look on the web for the guidelines here. Do bear in mind that if you opt to take the package and do not return to work, you will need to repay the extra money that you've been given.

When you decide to tell your school that you are pregnant is up to you – but you must inform the Head in writing no later than the end of the fifteenth week before the week your baby is due. The same goes for expectant fathers.

Most pregnant teachers have very positive experiences in school – you may even find that the kids are nicer to you and that they show a huge amount of interest in your state of blooming! However, should you encounter any problems or instances of discrimination, speak to your union rep immediately. The following tales show just how different head teachers can be in relation to pregnant colleagues:

The Head at school is great. He is very approachable and when I told him that I was pregnant he was fully supportive. He always came to ask me how I was doing and then, when I had the baby, he put no pressure on me to decide when I would be back.

Our Head is really supportive but during my second pregnancy the school lost a lot of staff. I do remember him pestering me a bit as to whether I'd be back full time or not after I had the baby – and this was when I was only twenty weeks pregnant! I stuck to my guns and said I'd tell him once I'd had the baby. It's important to know your rights.

I hadn't been at my school for very long when I fell pregnant and I didn't tell anyone. My Head of Faculty did my interim Performance Management Review and he was really pleased with the work that I had done, particularly in raising the profile of the department. He said he'd put me forward for a pay rise accordingly and that there should be no problem in having it approved by the Head – mainly because the same had been done for the male head of history the year before.

However, two weeks later he spoke to me again and said that the Head thought I was 'either pregnant – or soon would be, so no pay rise'! I was livid. Nor did I have any idea of how he'd come to this conclusion. Obviously it's illegal but with no union rep at our school I had to contact a solicitor. I've regretted ever since that I decided to take no action but I was too worried. Instead I intend to vote with my feet – I won't be back after my leave – but I wish I had the guts to really do something about it.

The last example here is clearly appalling – and thankfully very rare in schools. If something like this happens to you, then speak to the union, and remember that you can contact them directly if there's no rep at your school.

Onwards and upwards!

So, here you are: your second year under way, and probably flying past already. Hopefully by this stage you are experiencing the real rewards of teaching and the wonder that comes from actually helping young people to get the most that they can out of life. It's a privileged position to be in. Give it your all and be the best that you can be. And with reference to the quotation that began this book: **Cleanse those doors**. Good luck!

'You come across some great kids' names – Isaac Cox and Chris Peacock are two of my favourite examples of parents who just weren't thinking.'

Chapter 9

Tales from the front line

Whilst I was researching information for this book, lots of teachers told me stories of their first couple of years in teaching. Many of these were very useful for illustrating certain points that are made during the book and for giving advice – but there were several other tales that were far too memorable, amusing or morale-boosting to be left out. The following collection includes these stories.

'Being in secondary school you're always a target for flirting students. One boy in my NQT year had a real thing for me and used to stalk me around the school. When I went to my car one afternoon there was a piece of paper left on the windscreen with a "poem" written on it. I didn't know whether to laugh or get a red pen to correct his spelling mistakes and hand it back to him:

God mad butter
God mad cheez
God mad u 4 me 2 squeez

Delightful!'

'I clearly remember my first class with a Year 10 group who were mentalists. I had to go out of the room to get them some exercise books, and when I got back one of them had locked me out! I remember thinking that I should stay calm about the situation as the same thing had happened to a friend of mine and he went bonkers, hammering on the door and shouting, whilst the class fell about with mirth inside. I tried the handle twice as they observed me through the glass panelling and then I went to get my HoD, who looked in on them and demanded that they open it. Thankfully they did, but my confidence took quite a blast after that and I dreaded every Tuesday afternoon for a while after!'

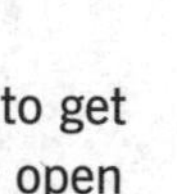

'My first day of teaching was the day after Princess Diana died. The school was awash with sobbing children and trying to do anything with my weeping Year 8s was impossible.'

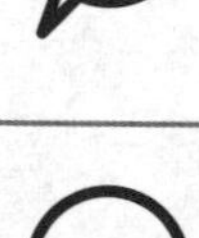

'Something that you never expect when you first go into teaching is the death of a student, but I've only been in the job for five years and it's been horribly and surprisingly common. You need to really compose yourself

and be strong for the sake of the kids at school – it's a horrible wake-up call as regards their own mortality.'

'Some kids at our school were doing their cycling proficiency tests and three of the boys had to be brought back in because they'd been mucking about on the road outside. The Head was telling them off when one of them did a massive fart. The other two kept a straight face, but not for long, and they all started sniggering. The Head walked off and left them to calm down – but how do you keep a straight face yourself during that?'

'I remember as a PGCE student something that always made me laugh and was a great morale booster at the time. I went to a wonderful first placement school, where I was introduced by the HoD as a teacher of music and not as a student. He encouraged me to always keep up this façade during my training year. So, when I went to my second placement, which was the worst school I had ever stepped foot in, I kept up the pretence. The school was awful, and the teachers were horrible and had no idea how to mentor students. The teacher who mentored me had previously taught in private primary schools and couldn't cope with a state secondary school. I sat one day at the back of her Year 9 class observing and thought to myself, "She can't control this class and yet she wants me to take them over in about three weeks' time!" I went on to teach this awful class for the next twelve weeks – it was pure hell and I nearly threw in the towel. However, when I announced to the kids that my placement was coming to an end they were gobsmacked – they said that they thought I had come to take over the HoD's role, who was retiring that same term! I was absolutely flattered and it gave me such a boost following the most awful five months of my life! It was all worth it!'

‘I was walking past the school canteen one morning and had a pair of flip-flops on. I stepped on a muddy wet patch and off I went, sliding on one flip-flop for several feet along the ground – a bit like an ice skater. I managed to stop myself from falling over, but realised that the incident had been witnessed by a group of boys who sat there, sniggering into their breakfast. The upside to this is that at least they see you’re human!’

‘We had an “activities week” at my last school which meant that just before the end of the summer term the entire school took part in an activity of their choice. I had been signed up for a residential trip to France but was being romantically – and persistently – “pursued” by the male teacher who was organising it. I had no wish to go away and take up his kind invitation to share his bivouac, so managed to get swapped to an in-school drama club for the week. Just before it began my partner and I discovered that we were expecting our first child, so I was even more relieved that I wouldn’t be spending my time in a raft on white water rapids. I did however have to spend the entire week in a blacked-out drama “studio” the size of a mousehole, that reeked to high heaven of teenage FEET, and that was packed to bursting with grumpy kids who were expected to spend the week enacting *Aesop’s Fables*. The fact that it was also boiling hot did nothing to curb my morning, noon and night sickness, and I was no use to anyone – I spent most of my time wilting in a chair and sloping off to the loo. The following year I made sure that I signed up early to an activity that I actually wanted to do – but the smell of those feet is with me still!’

‘In my second year we had a new Year 7 cohort and I had some memorable groups to teach. One of the boys had a sister who was older than him and had only made it through to Year 8 before she was taken out of mainstream schooling. The boy was pretty odd himself. He didn’t exactly misbehave, but he listened to nothing – even during one-to-one contact. He seemed to be on a different planet.

A few weeks into term it came to light during our staff briefing that this boy had decided to tell other members of Year 7 that he had fornicated with his cat – and that this "news" had spread like wildfire throughout the school. His poor tutor had to actually stand up in briefing and ask us to stop any Year 11s from meowing at him in the corridors when they passed him, as he was very upset about it. He had apparently thought it would be funny to lie and say he'd had sex with a feline but now of course it was backfiring somewhat.

A few weeks later I was teaching him during a lesson about reincarnation. I sat down with him and discussed the concept and asked what he would like to be reborn as. He started to give this some consideration and was quite responsive – I thought perhaps I was making progress – until I decided to tell him what I would like to be reborn as. The first thing out of my mouth before I could stop myself was the word 'CAT', and he looked like he'd been zapped by a thunderbolt. I tried my hardest to take it back but clearly he thought I was taking the mickey. Two weeks later my laptop was nicked from my desk and his mother turned up with it at school having found it in his room – I was obviously being punished by him for my "insensitivity"!'

'Before I got married I went on a diet, and my class kept asking me how it was going. I think it was meant to make me feel better when they said, "You're not fat, Miss, you're just a bit Christmassy!"'

'I don't "do" sick, I am sick phobic, and I assumed that by being a secondary school teacher I'd escape a lot of it, but no – I've had them puke in plastic A4 pockets because that's all I've had available, I've had them throw up on my classroom steps, and I've had them puke in a backpack. Why me?'

'I made some great friends during training. During my first PGCE placement I was at a school with a couple of other students from my university. One of them, Eleanor, was an MFL student, and I asked her to keep me abreast of anything her mentor was doing because mine seemed a bit dippy and I didn't trust her to get all of the paperwork done on time. In fact, she even managed to get my name wrong and kept calling me "Charity".

Eleanor had always been really lovely to everyone, including cleaning staff, and when our placements came to an end she was given a Christmas card by the cleaner of her room. It transpired that I wasn't the only person whose name wasn't remembered correctly because the cleaner had been mistaking Eleanor for a man for the past three months – she was presented with a card addressed to "Alan"! We were in stitches about it at the time and have been known to one another as Charity and Alan ever since.'

'We recently taught our Holocaust unit at school. The kids have to make a creative response to the concepts that we explore. One of the pieces handed in astounded us, but not in a good way. The student who had made this particular item had put a huge amount of effort into his work and had been extremely sensitive during lessons to the issues that we were dealing with – he simply didn't realise how inappropriate his piece was. He had made an interactive gas chamber.

By painting a box black and stitching together a tiny cloth corpse to lie in it, he had then painted and attached a can of Lynx to the side of the box. This sprayed directly into the box and onto the "person", simultaneously choking all around with the smell of deodorant. Teachers from all over the school heard about it and some were taking photos on their mobiles – this was after school of course as no one wanted to hurt the student's feelings! We just had to explain to him why his creative response was so very wrong on so many levels. It became worse when a week later we had German visitors to the school and all of our rooms were still stuffed to bursting with images of Hitler and Nazi paraphernalia. Mortifying.'

'I remember being on a placement when there was a fire alarm. The students all lined up on the tennis courts and we had to stand with our class. The Head came out using a megaphone and wearing her leopard print PVC overcoat, which was a sight to behold in itself. She started yelling into the megaphone about how the kids weren't quiet enough and as she did so some of my Year 10s started creasing up. I looked around and saw that a pigeon was emptying its bowels from a great height all over the back of an unsuspecting PE teacher. The Head had no idea what was going on and continued to go ballistic, her voice getting higher and squeakier in the megaphone. The longer it continued the harder it became to control myself – my shoulders were shaking, tears were streaming down my face and the PE teacher was still clueless. A classic, if unprofessional, moment.'

'A teacher in my department used the film *Boyz in the Hood* to teach about violence. He always fast-forwarded over an explicit sex scene and would turn the TV round to face him by the door whilst he did so. Not only did the Head walk past and look in on one such occasion (the doors have glass panels in them), but the kids later told me that the entire scene was always reflected in the glass anyway so that they saw the lot!'

'I keep in touch with a few ex-students and remember the first time that a couple of them said I had inspired them to go to uni and become teachers themselves.

It's an amazing feeling to know that you really do have an impact on people's lives.'

'When I left my first school and moved on to a new one, I was devastated to leave my tutor group behind. I'd had them since Year 7 and would miss their final year. I was really excited to be invited back to their leaving prom and it was very emotional seeing them again. I assumed they'd have forgotten about me as a hectic twelve months had gone by for them, but they even gave a speech about our times as a tutor group and presented me with a gift. One of the boys had been banned from the prom due to his behaviour, but he had a card and a present that he passed on to one of his friends for me. I had no idea until that moment that all the hard work and effort had meant so much to them. It was an incredible moment to see them all again and I will never forget them.'

Chapter 10

Useful websites

The purpose of this chapter is to help you plan and save time. Included are some really useful websites with contemporary resources and practical, engaging ideas that can be used in your classroom.

General

http://www.tes.co.uk/ The Times Educational Supplement website

http://tre.ngfl.gov.uk/ The Teacher Resource Exchange (TRE) is Full of activities that teachers have created and is also fully moderated by specialists.

http://www.teachernet.gov.uk/teachingandlearning/resourcematerials/ Full of teaching resources, with more than 2000 lesson plans!

http://www.teacherresources.net/ Resources for teachers covering all ages and levels.

http://curriculum.qca.org.uk/ National Curriculum website.

http://www.qca.org.uk/default.aspx Qualifications and Curriculum Authority.

http://schools.becta.org.uk/ Advice for teachers on the use of ICT in schools.

http://www.thegrid.org.uk/learning/ Hertfordshire based resource, with information on assessment, and so on...

http://www.topmarks.co.uk/ A great website for searching the Internet for the best resources.

Primary

http://www.primaryresources.co.uk Free Lesson plans, activity ideas and resources for primary teachers.

http://www.teachingideas.co.uk/ Teaching ideas for primary teachers. This site contains lesson ideas, activities and resources, and they're *free*.

http://www.sparklebox.co.uk/ Thousands of free resources that you can print out, directly for Foundation Stage and Key Stage One.

http://www.woodlands-junior.kent.sch.uk/teacher/ Resources for primary teachers. (This is a school-run site.)

http://www.teachingpets.co.uk/ Teaching resources for primary teachers.

www.thebricktestament.com Fantastic website that depicts a vast number of Bible stories in Lego, very engaging.

http://www.mmiweb.org.uk/gcsere/ An excellent site with great advice and a lot of links to further resources for primary and secondary teachers. This is run by Paul Hopkins and is great for teaching RS.

http://www.classideas.co.uk/ An excellent site that you can order display and motivational ideas from.

http://www.firstschoolyears.com/ Early Years and Foundation Stage are both covered here.

www.bbc.co.uk/cbeebies/ Early Years and Foundation Stage.

www.bigeyedowl.co.uk/ Early Years and Foundation Stage.

www.underfives.co.uk

http://www.learnenglish.org.uk/kids/ A good source for stories.

www.crickweb.co.uk/ A primary resource site.

http://www.coxhoe.durham.sch.uk

http://magazines.scholastic.co.uk/ You need to subscribe to this.

http://www.logo.com/imagine/project_gallery/weather.HTM This site allows children to create a weather map.

http://www.bbc.co.uk/schools/typing/ A goat teaches the children to type properly, using the correct fingers for each key, and makes it fun.

Secondary

SEN

http://www.senteacher.org/ Resources for special needs teachers.

http://www.woodlands-junior.kent.sch.uk/teacher/ Resources for primary teachers. (This is a school-run site.)

http://www.teachingandlearningresources.co.uk/ A site for primary teachers supporting the NC in England and Wales.

Literacy

Poetry archive

http://www.poetryarchive.org/childrensarchive/home.do Here the poets themselves read their poems for children.

http://www.teachit.co.uk/ Library of English teaching resources.

http://www.newi.ac.uk/englishresources/ For teaching and revision resources.

www.focusonphonics.co.uk A great site for phonics.

Numeracy

ICT games

http://www.ictgames.com/ A fun site for numeracy games.

BBC Bitesize Maths Games

http://www.bbc.co.uk/schools/ks1bitesize/numeracy/time/index.shtml You can practice telling the time, multiplication, and lots more.

www.enjoymaths.co.uk/ Lots of numeracy worksheets and other materials.

www.tes.co.uk/teacher/brainteasers/index.asp/ Excellent brainteasers for starters or extension work.

www.emaths.co.uk/ Lots of numeracy activities, plus some for the interactive whiteboard.

www.n-yorks.net/curriculum/subjects/maths/info.html/ Lots of numeracy worksheets.

www.nrich.maths.org.uk/public/index.php/ Good for higher achievers.

Science

http://www.bbc.co.uk/schools/scienceclips/teachersresources/teachersresources.shtml Science resources for primary teachers.

http://www.realscience.org.uk/ News and science teaching resources.

http://science.nhmccd.edu/biol/bio1int.htm I use this for A-Level biology animations to help illustrate different concepts in class.

www.squashedfrogs.com/ Excellent for starter demonstrations.

Music

http://www.mtrs.co.uk/ Music teachers' resource site. Subscription required.

http://www.soundjunction.org/teacherresources.aspa Music resources.

History

http://www.schoolshistory.org.uk/teachersresources.htm
Resources for history teachers.

www.victorians.org.uk
A great online site for studying the Victorians.

www.ancientegypt.co.uk
A great online site for studying the Egyptians.

Modern Foreign Languages

http://www.ashcombe.surrey.sch.uk/curriculum/modlang/index_teaching.htm
Modern Foreign Languages teaching resources. (This is a school-run site.)

http://www.talkingdice.co.uk/default.asp
Excellent resources for MFL teachers, from nursery through to adult education including SEN ideas.

PSHE/Citizenship

http://news.bbc.co.uk/cbbcnews/hi/teachers/default.stm
Citizenship news-based lesson ideas.

RS/RE/Philosophy

www.thebricktestament.com
Fantastic website that depicts a vast number of Bible stories in Lego.

http://www.mmiweb.org.uk/gcsere/ An excellent site with great advice and a lot of links to further resources for primary and secondary teachers. This is run by Paul Hopkins and is great for teaching RS.

http://www.rsrevision.com/ Another great site. This is run by Paul Emecz, an RS teacher at the Arnewood School. He has a speciality in E-Learning and the site is an excellent resource for teachers and pupils.

www.youtube.com/ Wonderful for resources: 'Every Sperm is Sacred' is always a winner.

www.mrdeity.com

http://www.cleo.net.uk/resources/index.php?ks=1&cur=15/ Videos and keyholes for RE.

www.request.org.uk
A great website full of RE resources.

Art and Design Technology

http://www.paperscissorskids.com/ Lots of arts and crafts ideas.

Assemblies

http://www.schoolassemblies.btinternet.co.uk/ Assembly ideas.

http://www.teachingideas.co.uk/more/assemblies/contents.htm

http://www.assemblies.org.uk/

Displays

http://www.displayphotos.co.uk/main.php

Rewards

http://www.teachingideas.co.uk/more/management/contentsO2rewards.htm

http://www.schoolstickers.co.uk

http://www.primaryteaching.co.uk

Continuing professional development

http://www.tda.gov.uk/teachers/continuingprofessionaldevelopment/epd.aspx

Interactive whiteboards

www.cardiffschools.net/~roelmann/whiteboard/general1.html
An interactive resource site.

Union websites

www.teachersunion.org.uk (The NASUWT)

www.teachers.org.uk (The NUT)

www.askatl.org.uk (The ATL)

www.natfhe.org.uk (The NATFHE)

www.naht.org.uk (The NAHT)

Index